D1536523

PRAISE FOR *CHOICE POINTS*

"Choice Points *approaches the difficulty of learning with retention and application with penetrating sensitivity that bodes well for readers and colleagues."*

—*Norman L. Paul*
coauthor of *A Marital Puzzle,* author of *Pre-Marital Choices*

"I urge all of us facing key life choices to dive into this workbook, trust the process, and enjoy the pleasure of career and life as a result."

—*Joan Goldsmith*
consultant, author of *The Art of Waking People Up*

Choice
POINTS

Sherry

wishing you many

great choices

Enjoy!

Sydney Kee

November 2003

Navigate Your Career
Using the Unique
PaperRoom™ Process

Choice POINTS

Sydney Rice

DAVIES-BLACK PUBLISHING
Palo Alto, California

Published by Davies-Black Publishing, a division of CPP, Inc., 3803 East Bayshore Road, Palo Alto, CA 94303; 800-624-1765.

Special discounts on bulk quantities of Davies-Black books are available to corporations, professional associations, and other organizations. For details, contact the Director of Marketing and Sales at Davies-Black Publishing, 3803 East Bayshore Road, Palo Alto, CA 94303; 650-691-9123; fax 650-623-9271.

Cover art: © Keith Skeen/Images.com.

Davies-Black and colophon are registered trademarks of CPP, Inc. The PaperRoom, Results System, and Partnership Pact are trademarks of Sydney Rice.

Visit the Davies-Black Publishing Web site at www.daviesblack.com.

Printed in the United States of America
07 06 05 04 03   10 9 8 7 6 5 4 3 2 1

Library of Congress Cataloging–in–Publication Data

Rice, Sydney
     Choice points: navigate your career using the unique PaperRoom process / Sydney Rice.
          p. cm.
          Includes index.

     ISBN 0-89106-173-8 (pbk.)
     1. Career changes—Decision making. 2. Career development. 3. Choice (Psychology) I. Title.

     HF5384 .R53 2003
     650.14—dc21

                                          2002035098

FIRST EDITION
First printing 2003

For Vinnie

Contents

Personal Inquiry Exercises

It is hard to let old beliefs go. They are familiar.

We are comfortable with them and have spent years

building systems and developing habits that depend

on them. Like a man who has worn eyeglasses

so long that he forgets he has them on, we forget that

the world looks to us the way it does because we have

become used to seeing it that way through a particular

set of lenses. Today, however, we need new lenses.

And we need to throw the old ones away.

—Kenich Ohmae
(Japanese guru to political and business leaders)

How to Use This Book

This book lays out a successful career navigation process called "The PaperRoom™" that I have used for coaching people for nearly a decade. Before the publication of this book, the PaperRoom exercise process took place exclusively in a 10' x 12' cream-colored room, empty at the beginning of the process except for two raspberry swivel chairs. If you were to come in and sit in one of those chairs in the center of the room—ready to start the same process you are about to begin in this book—you would be able to turn slowly and see a completely empty room with walls covered with sheets of fresh white paper, totally blank: thus, "the paper room." I would be there holding a tin filled to bursting with fat markers of every imaginable color, and we would begin to map your personal details, in a predetermined, organized way, on each sheet of paper. This book recreates for you the process that would take place in that room, your PaperRoom.

This is not a book in which you can skip to the "good parts" and forget about the rest, or barrel through to see how quickly you can get to the end. While readers have made rich discoveries throughout the book, the real prize for them has been in the last chapters. But if you have not done the work in the earlier parts of the book, you won't have the personal information, perspective, and understanding you will need to get the ultimate results. Each chapter builds on the last, and the value is in doing the suggested work in each and understanding why you are doing it. As you move through the book you will gain the tools that will finally put you in the driver's seat as you navigate your career/ life path.

A Systems Approach

The exercises in this book are "personal inquiries" designed to reveal patterns of thought and behavior that you may not have seen or whose depth of impact you may not have understood. These discoveries can go hand in hand with therapy, but they are not a substitute for therapy, nor will they interfere with therapy. Actually, this type of personal inquiry operates in quite a different realm. This book uses a systems approach to looking at your career, and as such the exercises will help you discover your ways of doing, seeing, or feeling about things that you have not noticed but that are influencing your results and quality of life. Sometimes the discoveries people have made in the PaperRoom reveal information that was not revealed in therapy, and sometimes specific areas are uncovered that would then benefit from the therapeutic process.

Timing Is Everything

It might help if you can think of this book as something more structured and guided than a journal, but less structured and more reflective than a workbook. Finding the pace that works best for you will give you the maximum benefits from the process.

In this self-driven process, the simple act of staying with it will result in a change in your thinking, a broadening of your perspective, and access to possibilities for your career that you couldn't have thought of before. Interspersed are stories of people who have created new careers for themselves after doing the PaperRoom. Plus, for the first time, the process is laid out so that you can discover the information you need to recreate your career on your own.

This book can be read in chunks, one chapter at a time, with days or weeks between chapters. You will be both learning and processing information, so giving yourself time in between will be useful. You don't need to tightly structure your "book time," though people who have done the PaperRoom have found that designating a regular time of day, at a particular time each week or month, seems to work best.

Forming a Book Group

I strongly suggest that you consider forming a group to work through this book together; your insights and the possible value for you will be enhanced greatly by hearing others' perspectives. Besides, you'll have a great time! Groups that have worked through the book have reported that most chapters and the accompanying exploration exercises take about a week each, though individuals may move along at a faster pace. Groups of three to five people find that two- to three-hour meetings seem to work for them on average. For more information see the appendix, "Guidelines for Starting a Book Group."

Book Design

We have used several devices in the design of the book to help make the book easier to follow and more usable.

- Wide margins are provided to give you room to take notes. The space also contains quotes relevant to the material you are reading currently and midchapter questions inviting you to pause and reflect on ways that the topic being discussed might apply to you.

- Personal inquiry exercises, found generally at the end of chapters, are used to guide you through the process.

Book Format

The book is divided into three parts—Scan, Focus, and Act—mirroring a device that is sometimes used for strategic planning. What better topic for strategic planning than the career focus of your life? Chapters in part 1, "Scan," review the context and content of your current and past work/life. In part 2, "Focus," you discover your core needs and values. In part 3, "Act," you bring all your learning together and start moving. Each of the book's ten chapters provides insights and tools that build on those of the preceding chapter.

Acknowledgments

The creation of this book has taken nine years of stops, starts, and resurrections. I can't imagine that any book could be a completely solo enterprise; this one certainly wasn't. Support and contribution from a group of very special people aided each stage along the way. Each person seemed to somehow arrive on the scene at just the right time and was an integral part of my learning how to replicate a process that had been delivered only orally by trained facilitators into a written process that people could do on their own.

Yuston Wallwrap, the advertising guru, was my first mentor/ coach, convincing me that I did indeed have a book and starting me on my way. Lauren Shusler-Shure did a beautiful job on the first interviews and in encouraging me to keep writing. Virginia O'Brien masterfully smoothed the early rough edges to create form and flow so that the book that was to be could finally emerge. My wonderful editor, Connie Kallback, steadfastly and with great good humor championed this book. Her attention to detail and nuance is a true gift.

My efforts would never have reached "book status" without Holly Whiteside, my extraordinarily talented writing partner. Her astonishing abilities to listen acutely, organize adeptly, and write beautifully helped me articulate my book in my own voice.

Synergy is usually thought of as 1 + 1 = 3. Working with Holly, it's more like 1 + 1 = 7 or perhaps 9. I'm thrilled that she has found her calling through our work together and that others will have the benefit of her "book midwifing" gifts.

The initial layout and design were brought to life by Marlene Andrews-Gilboy, whose only directive was "How the heck do I make this thing interactive?" The beautiful graphics are the work of Sandra Cohen, who had no idea what she was getting into when she innocently called one afternoon to get some coaching.

Thanks also for: support and contribution from Lucinda Lindy, Robin Bullard Carter, Una McMahon, John Whiteside, Mary-jo Porcello, Lisa Quiroz, Susan Foley, Jill Fallon, Joy Reo, Bob Elliott, and Wendy Sutherland, who were interviewed for this book; invaluable feedback from the test-run reading groups "Laura's Turtles" (Laura Tourrtellot's book group: Pat Hoskins, Barbara Donohoe, Tina Gleisner, and Donna Boyt) and "Joe's Band" (Joe Moran's book group: Neil Gibbons, Cheri Carlson, Karen Wager, Randy Pessin, Jones Paul Wing, and Marlin Kaufman), as well as the individual test-run readers, Jan Athos, Diana C. Libby, Susan Nash, and Gay Schoene; the tireless research done by Maureen Moran; and encouragement along the way from myriad others—Carol and Bob Frenier, Joyce McClure, Joan Sweeney, Jill Fallon, Ellen Kanner, Phoebe Ann Neiswenter, Helene Matzman, and my terrific son and daughter, Dan and Laura, to name just a few. Last, but most certainly not least, thanks to my wonderful husband and life partner, Vinnie, who unfailingly believes in me even when I forget to believe in myself.

About the Author

Sydney Rice, M.Ed., has more than twenty-five years' experience as a professional business coach, facilitator, consultant, and trainer. Founder and president of The Boston Coaching Company, Inc., she has worked with more than 2,000 individuals and more than two dozen organizations in a variety of settings. Clients have included BankBoston, the Boston Police Department, Chase Manhattan Bank, Harvard Community Health Plan, Cri-Tech Manufacturing, Thomson Financial, and Time, Inc.

Through her coaching practice, Rice recognized the need to provide leaders and organizations with a structure that would enable them to maintain their professional edge by enhancing their ability to leverage their strengths, develop future leaders, and successfully navigate change. The Boston Coaching Company provides leaders with individualized coaching and organizations with BCC Leadership Coaching Programs, customized internal Web site–accessed coaching and mentoring. Its team of eighteen senior coaching professionals resides in the United States and England.

Rice is the creator of the Partnership Pact™, a collaborative coaching and mentoring model that has been effectively employed by groups and individuals in a variety of organizations experiencing the need to both embrace new knowledge and retain traditional wisdom. She also designed The PaperRoom, an innovative process that provides individuals with the tools to optimize their effectiveness and make career choices that are personally and professionally fulfilling. These processes have proven beneficial and practical for executives, entrepreneurs, professionals, and creative artists.

Introduction

Many of us are finding that "the way it has always been" is too confining. We want more breadth and depth in our careers. Often we feel overworked or powerless, and our old skills for navigating aren't getting us where we need to go. We see our personal standards compromised for the sake of the bottom line, our productivity falters for lack of professional fulfillment, and, regardless of age or level of accomplishment, many of us feel frustrated.

As this new century began to unfold, so did a new urgency to question what we value, what we honor, and what we hold dear. The economic picture became an ever-changing image that we were hard-pressed to bring into focus. Collectively we reached a "choice point," a time to review and reevaluate the quality and direction of our future and the workability of our business practices. It was not possible for those who went before us to tell us what to expect, what to do, or who to be. It had become clear that the world they grew up in no longer exists and that the new world doesn't play by the old rules. We needed a new approach to working and living, and new navigation skills to serve us in today's world, which leads us to *Choice Points*.

Regardless of your level in your organization or whether you are self-employed, feeling professionally stuck or at a major crossroads, or working harder and enjoying it less, this is the book for you. But launching another career shift or taking aptitude tests or even finding work based on the strengths in your résumé is putting the cart before the horse. Maybe the problem and its solution aren't "out there," in the company, community, or family, the ever-present "other" wherein all opportunity, responsibility, and blame rest. Perhaps the answer is in us, in the way we think, the way we are used to doing things, and that's the good news—that we can do something about it.

Where Are You?

Consider for a moment that our habitual understanding or way of thinking is actually what is blocking our ability to see the best direction to take and how to begin. Much of the difficulty we are experiencing is due to our approach, our historical ways of doing things and succeeding. This faulty approach is based on the notion that stability (read: safety) means not changing, or changing only in predictable, time-proven ways. *Webster's Dictionary* defines stability as "the strength to stand or endure." In this book are tools to help you stay standing in a changing world. You will learn to choose change rather than let change choose you. The concepts and exercises presented here will help you uncover the specific perceptions, beliefs, habits, expectations, and assumptions that have been blocking you and provide you with new practices that will enable you to stretch beyond your past limitations.

In addition to our concerns about change, there is another problem complicating our professional lives: time. We say we don't have enough of it. But is that true? It may be on a given day. But we need to take another look at time. The habit of always looking to the past to inform us has limited our ability to see the present. We do have more time. We will live longer than our parents and be healthier as we age. Our lives simply are not as confined as our parents' (and their parents') lives were. We don't need to jam all that is important and vital into twenty or thirty years of adulthood and then coast. We don't have to peak at fifty only to descend rapidly into our dotage. Fifty is a new plateau for doing many different, meaningful things that can last well into our eighties. We don't need to do them all at once. And that reality has implications for each step we take toward making our work and life flourish. *Choice Points* introduces a new way to look at the stages of life that better reflects your current reality and allows you to take better advantage of this new reality and the opportunities it brings.

Where to Go from Here?

What might new rules for career and life design look like? Does having a career mean you do the same kind of work or stay in the same industry for life? What is wrong and what is right for you? What are your real priorities? What might it be like to work differently or to work at different things in the early years of raising a family? At what point do you choose to retire, and what could that mean? Doesn't *retire* mean to lie down? Retire *to* something, perhaps, but not retire. Our perspective of life is shifting as our thoughts turn increasingly to the way we are living, the results of the choices we have made in our work, in our relationships, in every domain of our lives.

Through sixty years of personal experience and fifteen years in my own coaching practice, I have learned that life seems to prepare each of us uniquely for our appropriate next steps. If we don't recognize or accept these unique opportunities, we lose something incredibly valuable, both to ourselves and to others who would reap the benefits. This is it—our chance to seize the moment, take a chance, and discover anew what we are capable of becoming. The value cannot be underestimated. It is the difference between a life that, as Shakespeare says, "creeps in this petty pace from day to day," and one that we can truthfully welcome each morning. We just need a few new tools.

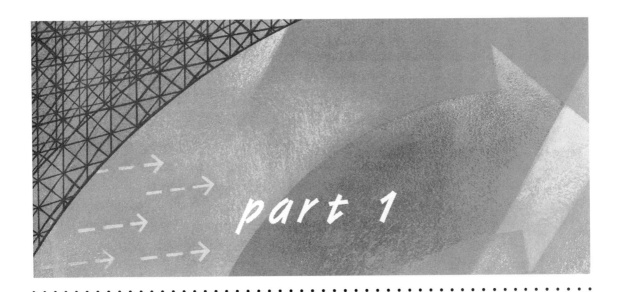

part 1

SCAN

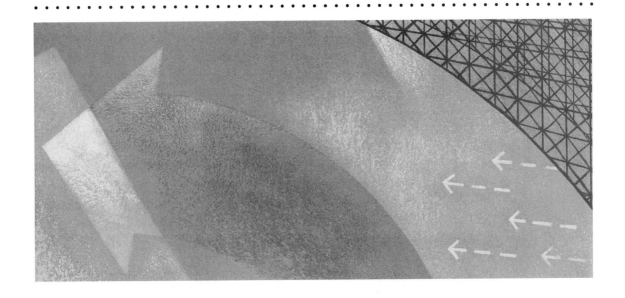

CHAPTER ONE

The PaperRoom™

I describe the PaperRoom™ as an episode of This Is Your Life. *The process says, "Here's the box you've been working in; this is who you are, so now you can go beyond it." Since doing the PaperRoom, I can see important choices I made without even knowing I had made them. For instance, I'm conscious of the people dynamics of work situations in a way I never was. For my entire career I've been a business architect, but what I hadn't realized was that the people element hadn't been integrated into my projects. Missing the people part broke quite a few projects. — Jeff*

In this first of four Scanning chapters you will:

- *Learn the upside and the downside of your invisible Results System™*

- *See the stumbling blocks and defenses that have been keeping your Results System in place*

- *Name the things you think have been stopping you*

Beginning Your PaperRoom

Ever wonder why all those good ideas you hear in seminars or read about in books are difficult to apply when you get back to work? Ever been frustrated because people don't "walk the talk"? Ever wonder what happened to last year's New Year's resolutions when it comes time to make new ones again? There are four good reasons we don't do what we promised ourselves we would:

- We don't remember

- It takes more time

- It's no fun

- We don't practice the new behavior long enough for it to become a habit

Behavior is what we'll be talking about in this book. Coupled with this discussion are tools to help you understand patterns in your own behavior of which you've never been aware. How would you like to: (1) release yourself from old constraints more easily so that you don't sabotage new resolutions, and (2) recognize what to do when you need to restore your confidence so that you can reach beyond what has limited you in the past?

The new insights and tools between these covers will let you create a career for yourself that is truly worth getting up for each morning. This process works. It has been developed and individually tested on hundreds of people for nearly a decade. These are people who were at a professional crossroads, people who were stymied about what to do next professionally or who, try as they might, kept coming up short on success or fulfillment in their work or career.

Reasons for Staying Stuck

One reason that you've never discovered the information we're about to uncover is that, like all of us, you have what I call a "Results System™." It is a kind of automatic thinking that helps you remember how you have done things in the past. Each time you do something successfully, your Results System files away information about how you have achieved success. That particular way of doing becomes, for you, the "right" way, so you repeat that way of doing something over and over, automatically. Without having to think or remember how, you just do it. Much like learning to ride a bicycle or drive a car, after a while you don't have to think about how to do it, you just do it. You run on automatic. That's all fine until you want to change, or the world around you changes, and you need to do things differently. In times requiring change, the automatic nature of your

"All my life I've wanted to be somebody. But I see now I should have been more specific."
—Jane Wagner, writer and producer

"Curious things, habits. People themselves never knew they had them."
—**Agatha Christie, author**

Results System stops you cold. Over and over I've seen that the very same system that has made us successful is the system that keeps us stuck.

Another reason you may not have seen the things you are about to discover here is that our usual way of figuring things out doesn't work for this particular discovery process. Generally, when we want to solve a problem or figure things out, we do it in our head. The problem here is that simply comparing one thing to another cannot reveal the information we are looking for. We need to be able to see the dynamic interaction of several things as they influence both our perception of a problem and the choices or options we think we have to solve it. This system of influences and perceptions is too complex to let us see all of it at once in a linear way. The exercises in this book will teach you how to gain access to that complex network of influences so that you can discover what you did not know you knew, and what you didn't know you didn't know. (Stop and let that sink in for a minute.)

Like looking in the viewfinder of a camera that opens up for a panoramic shot, you will "see" more—and have more data to choose from. You will have more choices so that you can take actions you had not considered, actions that will give you new results. You will also have at your disposal a defined practice that you can follow again to get the results you want in your career and life when you want them. Let's begin.

The PaperRoom: Setting the Scene

So, why are you here?

_____

_____

_____

_____

_____

"So, why are you here?" I ask you.

You move to your raspberry swivel chair. I hold my tin of fat colored markers, and we begin.

"What I'm going to do is explain the Results System so you can understand exactly what we are going to do, why we are doing it, and what the goal is. Then we will go to each wall. On each wall there is a long, wide panel, making a total of four panels. Each panel will present a particular aspect of, or window into, your life. I'll ask you questions, you'll give me the answers, and I'll write them on the wall. Don't be concerned if you don't think you have the answers. I'll help you.

"When we get to the end of the questions on the third wall, we're going to start translating this information so you can understand what the material we have gathered means for this process and how you are to use it. Next we will do the last wall, and then we will talk about how all the material in all four panels interrelates. Your job during the process is to make sure you understand what each section is for and to answer each question as truthfully as you can."

Good News/Bad News: Your Invisible Results System

People talk about changing themselves or their lives as though that were something they should be able to do easily. So if all the how-to books in the world really work, how come we keep buying them? There are two answers. The first is that it takes only a moment to intellectually understand a new concept—how or why something should be done differently—but it takes much longer to change our habits.

The second is that we all have an internal "Results System," an invisible system for repeating tasks, manners of doing or thinking about things as we have in the past. It helps us produce consistent results without even thinking about it—but it doesn't work in our favor when what we want is managed change. Here's how it works.

The best way to look at the Results System model (see figure 1) for the first time is to read it backward, from right to left. It shows that we seem to get:

What are some of your habits that affect your career?

_____

_____

_____

_____

_____

- **Results** because we took certain . . .

- **Actions** based on . . .

- **Choices** we made from what we felt were our available . . .

- **Options** based on our conscious or unconscious . . .

- **Goals**

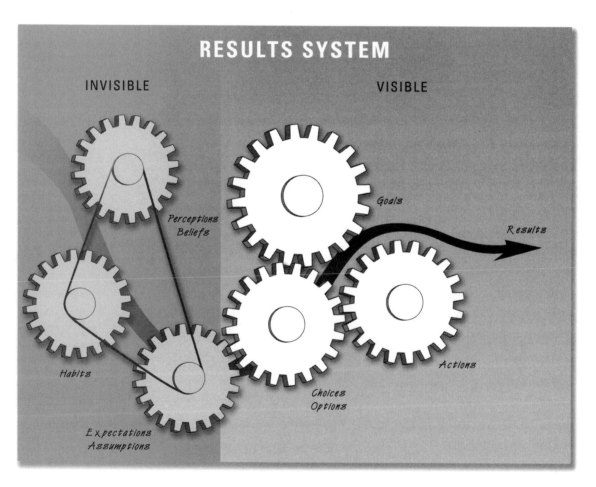

Figure 1 • Results System

This is the part of decision making we are aware of, and as a system it generally works pretty well. The only two times our Results System fails us are when: (1) we can't seem to get clear enough about what our choices, options, or goals are so that we can take the appropriate action; and (2) regardless of the changes we try to make, the result ultimately looks the same. We find a new job that finally makes us happy in our career, but eventually the new job starts looking like the old one.

When we are stymied about moving forward or find that regardless of our changes the result looks the same, it is because we have not delved into the invisible part of our Results System to make changes. We need to look at the next set of gears:

- **Perceptions:** how we see it

- **Beliefs:** what we believe about it

- **Habits:** how we have done things before

- **Expectations:** what we anticipate will happen

- **Assumptions:** what we suppose to be true about the results

While we are generally aware of about 80 percent of the visible part of the system, we are pretty much in the dark about the invisible gears. We are aware of some of our perceptions, beliefs, habits, expectations, and assumptions, but for the most part we refer to these bits as "is-isms," as in "this *is* the way it has to be done" or "this *is* what's wrong with that person." We are often oblivious to the possibility that we might have choices in what we think, how we see and hear, and how we act or react.

The Good News This Results System is an excellent system for keeping us safe and out of danger. You will marvel at its sophistication and strength as you get to know it, and you will see that

"Our life is not so much threatened as our perception."
—**Ralph Waldo Emerson,** essayist and poet

What "is-isms" are true for you?

_____

_____

_____

_____

_____

much of it is very useful. The invisible part of the system ensures that we repeatedly get the same results in situations that appear to be the same to us, and it can quite literally save our life.

To see its value, you only need to remember when you first learned to drive a car. Think about all the things you had to remember—gears, clutch, signaling, how hard you needed to press on the accelerator and the brake, how and when to use the rearview and side mirrors, and so on. Do you consciously think about all those things when you drive today? When you were learning to drive could you even conceive of talking to your friend, adjusting the radio, and eating a sandwich—simultaneously while driving your car? How is that even possible? Or how about knowing how to walk, do errands, get to work, or be unself-consciously quiet in the library yet loud at a ball game? The invisible part of the Results System can keep us safe by making sure that we repeat the patterns and procedures we have successfully followed—and survived with—in the past. We simply couldn't live in today's world, or yesterday's for that matter, if we had to recall all the steps and actions for all the things we do.

The Bad News This internal part of the system is not rational. It has no concern for your intentions or quality of life. Its only concern is to keep you alive, and it knows how to do that because it has you do things the same way you did them in the past—and you are still here to tell the tale. Many decades ago, when change occurred more slowly, perhaps even over generations, it made sense for the system to have all the power—it runs us; we don't run it. But nowadays it's a different story; you only need to have tried to diet, stop smoking, or begin an exercise regimen to have experienced firsthand the challenges of initiating change. The problem arises in today's world because today really is not like yesterday and what was appropriate then is not necessarily what is wanted or needed now. We need to be more in charge of our own life, to be in charge of how, when, or even if we choose to do things differently, rather than always be at the mercy of a system rooted in the past. The exercises in this book will give you the tools to navigate more smoothly, more like a sleek schooner than a lumbering tug.

This is how Jan made the shift to navigating differently:

I used to spend a lot of time in my head, trying to solve problems that way, and when things didn't go well I'd get caught up in emotional reactions. I can now separate the emotion and the logic and work them together or separately as need be. Before they'd be mixed up together. Now I'm amazed at how cool I can be in a troublesome situation.

You see, I always knew that to get things done you had to break the rules and step on toes. And I always did what I thought was the best thing to do for the project. But now I'm much more conscious of being able to step back as an observer, more than ever before. I'm now able to keep my emotions in check—I can step away, take a long look at it, take a broader view, see it from the other's perspective. Now I'm in a much more powerful position.

The Stumbling Block of Invisibility It is the invisible part of the Results System that makes doing things differently so difficult. It is the reason new resolutions fail, new situations are uncomfortable, and new procedures are problematic. When we see senior executives not "walking their talk," we assume it's because they don't mean what they say. From time to time that may be true, but more often they have yet to acquire a new system of beliefs, assumptions, and habits—or even know that they need to—to go with their new resolve. I witnessed a wonderful example of this at an annual world conference of a well-known organization. It was ironic that the very purpose of that organization was to explore and question the beliefs, assumptions,

"It is easier to ignore the facts than to change the preconceptions."
—Jessamyn West, author

and habits of the global responsibility of businesses in a world of change. In the opening comments, the chairman acknowledged the uniqueness of the group. He congratulated the members, saying that the way this group had first chosen to meet was groundbreaking in and of itself—executives were encouraged to "bring their wives," and the wives were even to be included and "allowed" to have a voice in all the discussions. The problem? Many of the executive members were women who had brought their husbands! You can be sure his oversight was not overlooked for a moment.

Was he a chauvinist? No! Did he not wish to acknowledge the women members? Of course he did. In fact, it was because of him that there were so many executive women in the organization. He was simply an older man who had known all his life that the word *executives* meant men. His invisible assumptions and habits did not fit the current reality or his intention. We are not in the habit of reviewing our patterns of thinking and feeling and doing. We don't even relate to them as beliefs and assumptions. We blithely go on in our inimitable way in this quickly changing world, not even recognizing that we are tenaciously living today as if it were yesterday. What is it that keeps us from seeing this invisible part of our system?

> "We learn from experience that we don't learn from experience."
> —George Bernard Shaw, author

Knowing When Your Silent Partners Are Taking Over

We will call the invisible gears of your Results System your "Silent Partners." They include the way you habitually or historically see a situation: your perceptions and beliefs; your usual habits of dealing with or resolving specific issues; and the results you expect or assume you will get when you take specific actions. You may remember that we have a much less wordy way to refer to this—we call it "is-isms." This *is* the way it's done; that's just the way she *is*; this *is* it.

These assertions are not arrived at capriciously—we call it the way we see it because this *is* how it has always been or how it has always worked in the past. When we established these perceptions, beliefs, habits, expectations, and assumptions, they seemed to be sound and their correctness was supported by evidence. It's no wonder we aren't aware of them.

The Three Lines of Defense

Our Silent Partners have three behavioral lines of defense to keep us blind to their existence, to keep us from tinkering with them.

The First Line of Defense for Our Silent Partners We do not consciously think to question our process. If the situation appears familiar to us, we don't stop to evaluate how we're approaching it even if the context or situation has changed—new boss, new job, new employee, new partner or mate.

The Second Line of Defense for Our Silent Partners Doing something differently than we have done it in the past is uncomfortable. It doesn't feel right. If your company upgrades the software you depend on to do your work and you find it has completely different toolbars and features, it just doesn't feel right. In the same way, if we're forced to take a detour from our usual way of driving to work, it doesn't feel right; it seems to take longer, or, at the least, it is inconvenient. Others may dictate new procedures and we are expected to follow them, but often they make absolutely no sense. And when faced with choosing between the discomfort of change and the comfort of the status quo, our natural inclination is to stay with the status quo.

The Third Line of Defense for Our Silent Partners We "invent" a rationale for not changing. We tell ourselves something quite reason-

What are some of the times when you use "is" without question?

_____

_____

_____

_____

_____

"If we don't change our direction, we're likely to end up where we're headed."
—**Chinese proverb**

"Because we cannot accept the truth of transience, we suffer."
—**Shunryu Suzuki, Zen master**

able and believable as to why this is wrong and we shouldn't do it, or, at the very least, why we don't need to do it now. How many of us have spoken to a co-worker, or someone who reports to us, in a way that we know is less than optimal, while saying something to ourselves like "I don't have time to bother with the better way right now; I just need to get the job done"?

The good news is that you need not operate totally in the dark. Although our Silent Partners are invisible, we can learn to recognize certain signs, or "flags," that tell us when they have taken over.

Two Silent Partner Flags

There are two flags that signal when a Silent Partner has taken over. The first appears when, over time, you are repeatedly stymied about how to resolve a particular problem. You've employed your talent or general creativity, doing what you did previously to resolve similar problems, but nothing is working. Bottom line—what always worked before doesn't work now. The second flag is raised when you can only come up with reasons for why something cannot work—or, at best, ways it might work that have no appeal.

Silent Partner Flag #1—Terminal Dissatisfaction: The More Things Change, the More They Stay the Same We often notice flag #1 more easily in others, as when a friend has a string of relationships that ultimately all seem to look the same. Joe marries Jane, then divorces Jane for Jill. After a while the problems Joe had with Jane turn up with Jill. We may or may not have the Jane-and-Jill problem, but we all have similar scenarios in some part of our life. New jobs begin to look like old jobs or the problems we are having with the new boss look like the same kinds of problems we had with the old boss, regardless of our

Have you ever said something like "I don't have time to bother; I just need to get the job done?

_____

_____

_____

_____

_____

concerted efforts to "do it differently" this time. We blame it on bad luck, poor choice, unfortunate circumstances, "just the way things are." But what if the cause is none of those things? What if it is because *we* were not the ones making the decisions, but rather our Silent Partners?

Silent Partner Flag #2—Being Stuck: The Inability to Move On A fairly common example of being stuck is when you just can't seem to quit a job or get yourself moved from a job you don't want. If you remember, your Silent Partners of beliefs, perceptions of the situation, habits of doing things, expectations, and assumptions about the kinds of results you will get are all based in the past. It is always the case that when people are having trouble moving on, they simply have never done it before, or at least not in this way. You will have an opportunity to explore this much more thoroughly when you work on your "Patterns" panel in chapter 4. The short explanation is that when we are facing a situation, the choices we see available to us are filtered by our Silent Partners so that only some of our options come to mind. The reasons you think you won't be able to do something are not necessarily wrong—it is that there are other possible choices and options that you haven't yet considered.

Do the two Silent Partner flags sound familiar?

_____

_____

_____

_____

_____

A Little Guidance

Have you ever been unable to find the kind of job you want or to know exactly what you are looking for? You may be very clear about what you don't want, but everything you explore, and most every suggestion others enthusiastically offer as "what you should do," just don't feel right. Of course, if we haven't done something before, our (not so) Silent Partners are likely to offer up some logical reasons for its undesirability. But if we have never done it before, who's to say we wouldn't like it?

Skills-Based Job Search Changing professions or job focus is also often very difficult because finding the right kind of work (or hiring the right kind of employee) is generally based on skills rather than attributes and this narrows down the search considerably. Whole classes of possible alternatives never even make it onto the radar screen. For instance, say you worked as a manager for a company that manufactures adhesives and were good at running meetings, getting projects in on time and on budget, and prided yourself on typing a gazillion words a minute. If you followed current reasoning you most likely would look for a managerial job in a manufacturing company that optimally was in the same industry. In all probability you wouldn't consider going out on your own as a consultant advising small companies on efficient project management.

It's true that looking for a management position in another manufacturing company would be a good bet, but let's look for a minute at the attributes that contributed to your previous success. They include commitment to the job, listening, problem recognition and resolution, interpersonal understanding, and strategic orientation. And although it is not a selling point, typing a gazillion words a minute translates into evidence that you get a kick out of going way beyond the acceptable norm when you feel personally challenged.

Now let's suppose you've always had a hankering to be your own boss but never saw how to do that on your current career path. Might becoming a project management consultant be something to consider? It would capitalize on all your skills in a way that could be far more satisfying. You would need to do some fact finding, but it might prove to be less far-fetched than you thought. It might just be an exciting profession that would tap into your love of being personally challenged.

As you cross into your new future, your Results System needs an upgrade from its primordial beginnings so that it serves rather than restricts you. You can start by learning how to recognize your hidden beliefs, assumptions, and habits that have limited you in the past. Later you'll learn how to get the upper hand on this system so that you can run it, instead of letting it run you. Trust me! It works! Now let's do a little delving into what's been stopping you.

What are some of your skills, aptitudes, and hankerings?

_____

_____

_____

_____

_____

Knowing What Stopped You

We begin by looking at what you can now see, those times in the recent or distant past when you had the thought that a change might be important, but for one reason or another you didn't make it happen. Maybe you talked yourself out of it. Maybe you tried the best you could and just didn't get results.

Take out a piece of paper and label it "Things I've Wanted to Change." Draw a line down the middle from top to bottom. On the left side, list everything you can think of that you've at some time wanted to change, yet have never really addressed. These can include objects, experiences, and relationships, to mention just a few. Beside each one, write down what you think stopped you. You might want to include in the list:

- Things you want less of
- Things you want more of
- Relationships you'd like altered, and how
- Experiences you'd like to have
- Things you'd like to own

- Skills you'd like to have
- Things you'd like to stop doing
- People you want in your life
- People you want out of your life
- Changes you'd like to make to your environment

Later in the book we will refer back to your list and you'll see even more about what's been stopping you.

By now you have a picture of your Results System, and you can probably see some of the defenses that have kept it in place. You've also listed some of the roadblocks that have been keeping you where you are. In the next chapter you're going to begin to look at important decision opportunities in life known as "choice points." Then you will do an exercise that takes you more deeply into the roots of what stops you. You'll also begin to list the life goals, both short-term and long-term, that you'd like to achieve moving forward and your goals in reading this book.

CHAPTER TWO

Choice Points

I had been working in a company that was then bought by another organization, and things started to change. I put up with it for a while, but I became increasingly dissatisfied. Finally, I asked for a [severance] package. I went back to school, but then my father became ill and I had to drop out. So, to generate revenue, I started consulting. By default, I'd been making so many decisions that impacted my career; I didn't know how to differentiate a good decision from a bad one. I realized I needed focus badly, and that's what brought me to the PaperRoom. It was great; I was finally able to put together the pieces to be successful. — Maria

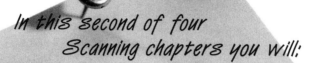

In this second of four
Scanning chapters you will:

- Learn about choice points in your career path
- Learn how to recognize your choice points
- Learn how choice points differ depending on your life quarter
- Discover the tool known as the "Progress Path of Change"
- Use the power of "why?" to get at the roots of a problem
- Create lists of your long-term and short-term goals

The Niggling Begins

The job begins to niggle. Irritations erupt at surprising moments. We begin to look at things differently than before. Something shifts. It's getting to be time to do something. For example, when it gets to be time for me to buy another car, I find myself checking out other cars on the road and being more aware of car ads—even reading them! It's not really a conscious thing; just some "getting to be time to buy a new car" switch turns on. I don't mean that I really have nothing to do with it. Something may have worn out, or my old car may not start up like it used to. But the gist of it is, it's time for a change.

What Are Choice Points?

In the fall of 2001, when I was completing the final touches on this book before submitting it to the publishers, I was still grappling with what the book should be named. What, exactly, was this book about? I know, of course, that people can and do change after doing the PaperRoom, but the book was about so much more than that. Then a friend invited me to a conference with Gregg Braden, an earth science expert. I just had a hunch there was going to be something there that I needed to know for my book. Sure enough, about halfway through the conference, he began to speak about something called "choice points." According to Braden, in 1957 Hugh Everett III, a pioneering physicist from Princeton University (and the man who developed the idea of parallel universes) wrote a paper in which he gave a name—"choice points"—to the moments in time when the course of an event may be changed. He explained that a choice point is like a bridge, making it possible to begin one path and then change course to experience the outcome of a new path.

But these opportune moments to redefine outcomes may come only at specific intervals where the roads of time *bend their courses* and approach other roads. Sometimes the roads become so close that they touch one another. One could easily make a choice at that point to continue the course to its inevitable end or choose to take another course all together.

Now, I know very little about physics or quantum theory—but this is exactly what I was looking for! This was the core principle of my book. There are points in our careers (and lives) when we know in our bones that if we are going to change, the time is *now*. These are the times when people have found their way to the PaperRoom, when they realize they want to make totally new choices that are not influenced by the past—such as Anita has done:

"One can always point to a time, a choice, an act that set the tone for a life and changed a personal destiny."

—Carol O'Connel, writer

These insights into what I need to be happy are so critical. There are so many paradigms for what it is to be successful that I forget to think about what makes me tick. For instance, I saw that I am not my mother (full-time mom) and not my father (very successful full-time professional), but I can define success on my own terms. It gave me license to throw away those icons and go my own route.

The Many Faces of Choice

Choices come in little packages and big ones, and we never seem to run out of them. They range from the insignificant, like when or if to have lunch, to life choices such as choosing a new job or new career. Some of our choices are logical and are greatly influenced by our environment, such as the kind of work that is available or what "people like me" do for a living. To some degree our age, gender, and level of education, as well as the expectations others have for us, all do their part in coloring our choices or influencing our need to make them. Sometimes the need to make a choice is out of our control—we were downsized, became ill, or had an accident; the organization folded; we were fired. On other occasions we choose to make a change because of our own agenda or needs. We choose a new path to make better money or to move our career forward more rapidly or to make more time for family. For example, Wilma had been doing everything right but one day found that her choice point had crept up on her when she wasn't looking:

Before I did the PaperRoom, I lived in a neat little house in a nice Connecticut suburb, commuted to New York City making loads of money, and was miserable. I had no community, had made no friends in three years. I was single, living in a married community. My job was high stress, giving very little pleasure, and I had no col-

"We all have big changes in our lives that are more or less a second chance."
—Harrison Ford, actor

"Dissatisfaction with the status quo can be a powerful force."
—Dorri Jacobs, organizational consultant

legial connections to speak of. And I hate the winter with a passion! All my inner resources were going to bringing home a paycheck. I had, on my own, applied for a job in California with my organization, but the job had been given to someone else. I entered the PaperRoom feeling fed up, stressed out, and drained. Though I could think of various options for my life, I wasn't sure on what basis to make a change in my life or which change to make. After all, I had followed all the rules for success and ended up miserable. Maybe I needed to base my next move on something different.

Many of us also feel the need to choose fundamental change when we embark on a new stage of life and the core focus of our professional life shifts to a new place. Many people in the earlier part of their adult life are generally looking to find the right place, literally and figuratively, to build their future and to take their place in the world professionally. This may require an initial stage of working through some personal challenges, but eventually we create our place in the world in some fashion. People at a later time in life will more likely want to move beyond, to discover how they can both contribute what they have learned in their work life and explore new challenges that integrate with their life as a whole. Each time of our life calls us to focus on a particular set of issues.

Our choice points announce each emerging shift of focus and the opportunity to choose to step onto a new path—or not. The exercises and processes in this book are effective, regardless of where you are in life or where your career focus for development or change is.

Recognizing Choice Points

Susan was facing the kind of choice point I often hear about from people in their thirties:

"Life is a succession of moments. To live each one is to succeed."
—Corita Kent, activist, teacher, and artist

What events have prompted a few of your choice points?

_____

_____

_____

_____

_____

Just before I found the PaperRoom, my life was highly in flux. Here I was, a business school graduate with a baby, no job—I didn't think I would ever find a job that fulfilled my needs. I was in touch with a lot of people, but nothing was clicking. I felt knocked off my horse. What was I going to do? I knew I really loved work; it gave me an important validation. But I could see the problems with working full time. It wouldn't be fair to my child. So I was just trying a lot of different things. I was on a defined path that wasn't a lot of fun. It was part of the growing and changing you experience when you have a baby. It's such a shock to your system, your lifestyle. You have to figure that all out. I learned why later. I hadn't leveraged what I liked or did best. I never felt, "Oh yeah! I can really get into this!"

Linda faced the choice point experienced by many at a time they would consider to be midcareer, at age forty-three:

I'd been assistant to the president for a company running projects in Saudi Arabia, I had my MBA, and I'd been the CFO of a nonprofit. And in 1990 I had this idea to start my own company as a financial advisor for women, helping them create a healthy relationship with money. Everyone thought I was crazy. It came to me in a canoe on the lake. The idea was so small I thought to myself, "I don't dare voice it or it will disappear." I held onto that idea and nurtured it. It just came into me so strongly. Finally, I had to put words to it, so I sat my husband down and made him just listen.

When John came to me, he had locked himself into his career. Everything was at stake and he was getting desperate, struggling to find a way out:

The last four years since my PaperRoom have been a time of enormous change. In '97 when I did the PaperRoom (I was fifty-five), I was working in my own consulting company, and was very fran-

tic about it, completely committed to it. It involved a tremendous amount of work and anxiety. I was doing everything I could to have it succeed, get ahead, make a difference in the workplace. And it was happening. In my first two years we grossed over a million dollars. Looking back, I was starting to get quite scared and unhappy with where I was going. I didn't know how much longer I could keep putting out.

As we begin to recognize the choice points in our lives and listen closely, we will hear a new voice, a different voice. We will recognize that it is time to take the next navigational turn to embrace all of what this next life phase offers.

Our Purpose in Life's Four Quarters

Up until now, life has been considered to be divided into three primary stages: childhood, adulthood, and old age. But with our expanded period of healthy years we have more time—much more time. Due to this increased duration of vitality, I now see life as having *four quarters*. The names I have given the quarters generally reflect the life patterns of my clients. Each quarter seems to have an all-encompassing "theme," "purpose," and "job." Of course, not everyone will follow this pattern exactly— feel free to adjust it for yourself.

Looking at life in quarters more closely reflects the current reality of our projected life span. It begins to give us a more realistic way to focus on what is important *now* and allows us to plot our lives more reasonably so that we can take full advantage of both the demands and the gifts of each distinct life stage. It simplifies things and overall gives us more room. As we go through the concepts and exercises in the remaining chapters, I will suggest that you look at your career using this construct. Remember, this is only a suggestion. Try

Life Quarters

Q1: Youth (1-25)
Theme: Education
Purpose: Learning the ropes of life
Job: Finding our place in society

Q2: Adult (25-50)
Theme: Creation and stability
Purpose: Providing for ourselves and future generations
Job: Building the future

Q3: Mentor (50-75)
Theme: Contribution & community
Purpose: Authenticity
Job: Fulfilling who we know ourselves to be

Q4: Historian (75-100)
Theme: Treasurers of the past; keepers of history
Purpose: Ensuring the continuum
Job: Teaching and sharing our historical perspective and wisdom

it on—and adjust the timing of the life quarters to make the construct work for you.

Life Quarter Quandaries

Each life quarter has its gifts and challenges, but because our "work life" or career takes place primarily in Q2 and Q3 we will focus on these two quarters in this book. We'll be going into more depth about these life quarters in chapter 5, but for now we'll focus on the core themes for Q2 and Q3, "creation and stability" and "contribution and community," respectively. These are the concerns most often brought into the PaperRoom. (This is due primarily to the fact that the average age of the more than six hundred people who have been through the process is 52.3 years, with most between the ages of 33 and 66.)

I first identified these themes just prior to my creation of the PaperRoom; the personal thoughts and concerns I had been noticing in my friends and clients, I had been experiencing as well. As I have watched clients move through the PaperRoom, I have continued to notice that we see our earlier professional years from a very different perspective than we do when we get older. Two things change—the circumstances in our lives and how we experience life—yet many of us seem oblivious to the change. No wonder we have trouble.

I began Q2 by getting married and moving from Los Angeles to Boston. I worked hard at the Q2 theme, "creation and stability," with its purpose of "providing for ourselves and future generations" and the job of "building the future." I had my children, worked at being a perfect wife and mother, explored and took on different kinds of work, learned different skills, and embraced a variety of responsibilities as I endeavored to discover and define who I was. My growth shifted and turned in this most complicated time of life. I often think that this time,

"Time is a dressmaker specializing in alterations."
—**Faith Baldwin, author**

particularly for women, is one of the most difficult as we try to define ourselves as professionals, mothers, and wives all at the same time. Even if we are not taking on all three at once, we seem to have all three choices hanging front and center in our closet of choices.

Q2 Issues Take a look at the following list of other issues facing many Q2 people:

- People who choose to leave the workplace to stay at home have problems with the transition.

- Those who choose to work, or must work, are torn between career and family; they have trouble balancing numerous activities, children, a spouse, a career, personal growth, and a sense of individuality.

- Single parents worry about raising a family alone, concerned they can't give their children a good upbringing.

- Divorcees and single persons are concerned about being alone and where and how to find someone new.

- Many in their forties feel that their thirties just passed them by and they did not enjoy them—they survived them; they focus on what they have not accomplished rather than what they have accomplished.

Societal Trends Impacting Q2 and Q3 Now let's look at how the following trends impact both Q2 and Q3 issues:

- In the 1960s and '70s, when one graduated from college he or she was expected to get married and start a family; now, many individuals are extending their education, taking time off before starting a career, traveling, etc.

Which of these issues are impacting your life?

_____

_____

_____

_____

_____

"The hardest years in life are those between ten and seventy."
—Helen Hayes (at 73), actor

- The average age for marriage has shifted from 24.3 years in the '70s to the late twenties to early thirties now.

- Because people are getting married later they are having children later; having babies in one's early forties is becoming commonplace, whereas in the late '70s it was rare.

- Families are smaller today; the average household size has declined from 3.14 people in the 1970s to 2.25 now.

- The number of one-parent families is increasing, and two-fifths of unmarried-partner households in 2000 included children younger than eighteen; the number of fathers getting custody of children is soaring.

- Many families are opting to have one parent stay at home to raise the children; today it is more common for men to want to be more involved in the daily lives of their children, so there are many more stay-at-home dads now than in the '70s.

- Divorce rates soared in the '80s and early '90s but leveled off in the late '90s.

- Since the 1990s, telecommuting has steadily changed family dynamics.

As you can see, in this new world we are just beginning to invent ways to make life work effectively for our families and organizations, as well as for ourselves. We are all, in a very real sense, the pioneers.

Una talks about life in Q3:

I've had a good career as a bookkeeper. But I've found in the last few years that I'm pulling back more and asking, What do I really want my life to be? I'm looking at who I am and what my life means for me. I'm recognizing that I'm in my fifties, and I expect that I'm going to have at least twenty-five more active years ahead of me. I'm looking at what I want and need to do to respect the life that I have or give the best of myself to the rest of my life.

Q3 Choice Point Transitions Transitioning into our third quarter is no easier than is working on Q2. It doesn't matter if you own your own business or work in a large organization, are professional or salaried or paid hourly. It doesn't seem to matter whether or not you have fulfilled your secret personal dream or reached your highest rung of success. Suddenly it becomes very important to take a new look at life. I love Jim's description of his career/life epiphany. Jim, a senior consultant, told me about an early spring day when he was walking home from his office and he paused for a moment to watch a group of kids playing tag. It triggered a powerful realization for him that the race to attain the corner office had lost its luster and was not worth the cost to his quality of life.

We may not have an epiphany like Jim's that propels us into a search for a new and deeper authenticity. It could just be that we see our workplace changing as new faces come in and the old, familiar ones move on. The need to make new choices sneaks up on us, and suddenly it becomes patently clear that "someday" has arrived. With some patience and creativity we can answer the question to Peggy Lee's plaintive song: "Is That All There Is?"

My own midlife defining moment occurred right on time, in the middle of my fiftieth birthday party. I felt detached, like I was a visitor rather than the guest of honor. I was frustrated with my inability to have a life that felt integrated, focused, purposeful, and authentic. It did feel as though I was almost there,

"We must become the change we want to see."
—**Mohandas Gandhi**

but it had been "almost" for an excruciatingly long period of time. I had reached the apex of an important choice point.

Recently there has been increasing literature affirming the reality and nature of our midlife changes. Judith R. Gordon and Karen S. Whelan, in their article "Successful Professional Women in Midlife" (*Academy of Management Executive*, 1998) indicate that women tend to make their changes incrementally, taking one step at a time. Ultimately they refine and rebalance their activities and priorities, which leads typically to new models of living. Men, on the other hand, often make major changes in work and family and may design a completely different life structure. The John D. and Catherine T. MacArthur Foundation Research Network on Successful Midlife Development has done exhaustive research on the myths of aging that support our experience of ourselves at midlife. They make it clear that the shift is not so much about getting "old" as it is about focus.

Boston Symphony conductor Seiji Ozawa told a story at a gathering for his sixtieth birthday that illustrates the point beautifully. He said that he had practiced music every day since he was a young boy, and that when he was younger he used to pride himself on the breadth of his musical knowledge. But as he got older, he found that it was not the breadth of music that interested him so much as its depth. He told of a teacher from his childhood who had told him there were pieces of music he wouldn't understand until he was much, much older, and he said he had finally seen this to be true. The metaphor is perfect. Only at midlife do we begin to have the experience and learning we need to refocus and refine our quality of life, but it is the result of all our previous experiences that makes that possible. Our life experiences only build on themselves; nothing is wasted.

The Progress Path of Change

When you find yourself at a choice point in an uncomfortable circumstance that you would not have chosen, how do you respond? Do you try to pretend nothing has changed and ignore the telltale signs? Do you face matters head-on? Do you act first and think later? Or do you carefully line up your ducks before moving an inch? Whatever your personal style has been, whatever your default strategies for coping with surprises, notice one thing: when old patterns and assumptions determine your actions, you are likely to get the same results as you have in the past. Our unconscious patterns can be reactions to our discomfort, rather than well-thought-out decisions and choices based on who we are now. Doing a competent job of making the right choices to change your career direction, or simply to live life differently, requires some measure of truth telling and bravery, and it always feels risky. One way to ensure that you will not put your new resolve unnecessarily at risk is to understand the process of change and to plan accordingly.

One of my most popular workshop handouts is "The Progress Path of Change," shown in figure 2. At the moment we first choose to commit to change in some important way, we are generally following a message from our gut or heart rather than our head. Although we know it feels right, we cannot be certain that it *is* right, and there is a time of frustrating discontinuity between our resolve to leave behind the "old" way of doing things and our knowing what will replace it. Facing this ambiguity straight on and not backing off until a new vision is realized takes patience, perspective, and persistence. Tenacity will make the difference between merely coping with work and having a job that is truly fulfilling and rewarding. The Progress Path of Change will help explain why you are feeling as you do along the path and suggests appropriate steps to take to move on.

When you find yourself at a choice point in an uncomfortable circumstance that you would not have chosen, how do you respond?

_____

_____

_____

_____

_____

"You don't just stumble into the future. You create it."
—Roger Smith, author

"We must act in spite of fear . . . not because of it."
—Anonymous

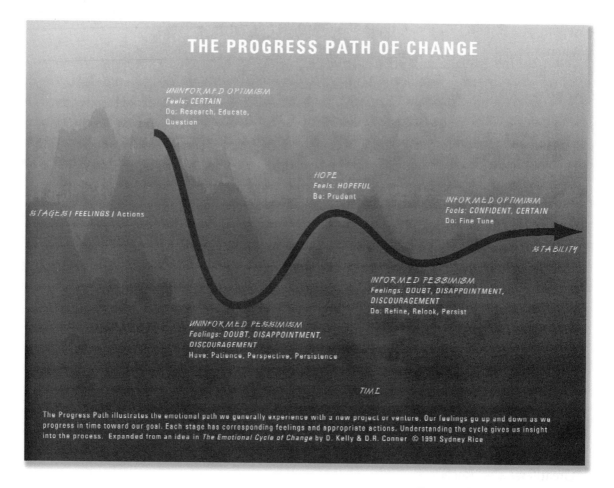

THE PROGRESS PATH OF CHANGE

UNINFORMED OPTIMISM
Feels: CERTAIN
Do: Research, Educate, Question

HOPE
Feels: HOPEFUL
Be: Prudent

INFORMED OPTIMISM
Feels: CONFIDENT, CERTAIN
Do: Fine Tune

STAGES / FEELINGS / Actions

STABILITY

INFORMED PESSIMISM
Feelings: DOUBT, DISAPPOINTMENT, DISCOURAGEMENT
Do: Refine, Relook, Persist

UNINFORMED PESSIMISM
Feelings: DOUBT, DISAPPOINTMENT, DISCOURAGEMENT
Have: Patience, Perspective, Persistence

TIME

The Progress Path illustrates the emotional path we generally experience with a new project or venture. Our feelings go up and down as we progress in time toward our goal. Each stage has corresponding feelings and appropriate actions. Understanding the cycle gives us insight into the process. Expanded from an idea in *The Emotional Cycle of Change* by D. Kelly & D.R. Conner © 1991 Sydney Rice

Figure 2 • The Progress Path of Change

Uninformed Optimism

The path begins at that moment when we commit to our new resolve. "This is it," we say. "I have the answer!" This first phase is called "uninformed optimism." We just know we are going to go for it. We feel certain. Unfortunately our euphoria is often fleeting. In the very next breath we are saying to ourselves, if not to others, "Am I out of my mind?" It seems to take only a second to be overwhelmed with doubt and fears about how—or even if—

we can actually do it. We feel disappointment, discouragement. When we make commitments from the heart, we often don't know how we are going to fulfill them. It is simply something that we need or want to do. The heart doesn't need to know the details.

Climbing the First Hill

The first hill on the Progress Path of Change is the steepest and the most difficult. It is the place where resolutions are broken and commitment weakens. Often it takes some time before you will have any evidence of success. The climb up the hill must be accomplished simply because you say so. Well-meaning friends and acquaintances may try to dissuade you. "You've given it a gallant try," they will say. You will doubt the wisdom of your resolve and feel disappointed and discouraged, but the keys to success are to have patience, remember to put things into perspective, and, by all means, persist.

The Second Hill

If we don't quit, eventually we get to the top of the first hill. "Great!" we say, "finally!" It is such a relief to see that the struggle was worth it, and that makes the next dip, heading for the second hill, even more devastating. It truly feels as if we are back at step one again. But notice how Kelly and Conner, who first described the Progress Path, named these low points: "uninformed pessimism " and "informed optimism." The second dip is not like the first at all, but it might *feel* the same. We actually are very much smarter. We have a vast bank of new data that we acquired on the way up the first hill. If we can manage not to settle for less than what we aimed for and keep on going a bit longer and a lot smarter, we can reach the top of the second hill and ultimately the goal of stability.

"I don't measure a man's success by how high he climbs but how high he bounces when he hits bottom."
—**George S. Patton, U.S. army general**

"Our repeated failure to fully act as we would wish must not discourage us."
—**Thomas Troward, divisional judge of the North Indian Punjab (1869 to 1896)**

Whenever we choose to make changes, this path applies. We all have been through it many times over. If you have ever decided to rearrange your workspace, reorganize your department, or buy a new computer, you have put yourself on the path. Predictably, getting through this book will at times seem to follow this pattern as well. It always looks like a good idea when we make our decision to go for it, and it takes a great deal of tenacity and persistence before we can really see that the struggle was worth it.

Look at it this way: it has taken you twenty-five to fifty years to have your life look the way it does now. It is not realistic to assume that you are going to change it overnight.

About Loss

I wish that it weren't so, but you can't have gain without loss. Of course, we like it when the loss is something we have wanted to get rid of. Then the sense of change reminds us of what we are only too thrilled to be without. But even if it were possible to just keep adding to the list of experiences in your life, continuing to do all the things you ever did in the past, each new addition would change your experience from what it was before. There is no getting around it—change equals loss of some sort, and your avoidance or reluctance to experience this discomfort is one of the major contributors to your reluctance to move on. What to do?

The first "solution" is to separate the new situation from your experience of loss and to deal with each separately. Celebrate your change and deal appropriately with your sense of loss. Don't just tuck the sense of loss away or avoid it—it will only come back to haunt you by diminishing your joy or highlighting the difficulties of the new situation. Not to overdramatize, but all loss or change is a sort of death. It represents closure

"Success is the sum of small efforts, repeated day in and day out."
—Robert Collier, writer

on whatever experiences were present before and closure on any hopes or expectations you might have then had for the future. Predictably, at some point you will go through the five stages of loss as recognized by Dr. Elisabeth Kübler-Ross, the well-known author of *On Death and Dying:* denial and isolation, anger, bargaining, depression, and acceptance. The biggest help is simply to understand that these feelings or emotions are normal and not to think that there is something wrong with you—or them—because you are experiencing them.

This is where ritual of some sort is a handy thing. What do you need to do to feel "complete," to acknowledge the loss in some formalized way? Are there people you should touch base with? What might you do to feel you have honorably put the past to bed?

The second "solution" is a great language trick I learned years ago in the *est* training: use the word *and* instead of *but.* "I have a great new job *and* I miss my old friends" rather than "I have a great new job *but* I miss my old friends." Using *and* lets you have both the new job and the experience of loss. When we say *but,* one negates the other—the good (new) is tainted by the bad (loss) and suggests you cannot have both.

Reminders

Reading and working with the "Personal Inquiry" sections of this book will take you through all the steps to the end of the Progress Path of Change. Have patience. Take your time. Put the book down if you feel like it; pick it up again when you are ready.

In the "How to Use This Book" section, I suggested that you read this book along with friends in a book group. If you are reading this book to truly change the quality of your life in some way, let me make that suggestion again. You'll want to share this time with others to get ideas and see other realities and perspectives through their eyes. In addition, the group can give you support for your journey. Others can question things you may not have seen and, more important, they can remind you of the progress you have made. Unless you have an unusual supply of support people in your life, this can be the one place where you are guaranteed consistent encouragement when your resolve weakens, and applause for your many successes. For help setting up a group, see the appendix, "Guidelines for Starting a Book Group." There is also some additional book group information at *www.thepaperroom.com*.

It will be helpful if you start a journal for the "Personal Inquiry" sections of this book. It is not a problem if you wish to do this in your head, or in a conversation with another, rather than on paper. But later on in the book when you have discovered some new things, you may want to revisit your answers.

Motivations and Goals

There are three steps to this personal inquiry. Step 1 is a powerful little exercise for getting to the heart of your motivations and what stops you. In step 2 you will look at what has ceased to matter or work for you. In step 3 you will get down to listing some of your goals.

Step 1 • The Power of "Why?"

Step 1 is an old and very simple exercise you may have used in the past. It is brilliant in its simplicity and never fails to reveal hidden obstacles to progress, even when applied to seemingly less-significant issues. Use the issue that first comes to mind, not necessarily the one that's most important. Even the things that seem simple can mask important motivations and learnings.

To begin, answer the following question and each "why?" that follows.

1. What have you been putting up with, or simply tolerating?

Why? _____

Why? _____

Why? _____

Why? _____

Why? _____

Example: *I've been putting up with the dogs (or co-workers) coming into my office while I'm working and bothering me. Why? I don't know! Why? Because, well, the poor things are lonely. Why? Because my office is part of the house and they own the house, too. Why? Because my office is part of the house and I have a responsibility to take care of my home. Why? Because my obligation to my home outweighs my obligation to myself. Because my office is part of the house (or company) and they are a part of it. Why? Because my obligation to others outweighs my obligation to myself. Why? Because I don't take my work seriously. Why?*

Because I haven't consciously designed my environment to support my needs and *live up to all my values. Whew! (That's eight "why?"s, but you can use as many as it takes to unmask your reason for doing something.)*

You can use this exercise to explore many elements of your life, both large and small. For each of the following questions use the same pattern—answer the question, and then question your answer five more times, each time taking the new answer to a deeper level. You'll know when you're telling the truth and when you're finished.

2. What would you like to change?

_____

_____

_____

3. What do you no longer want to tolerate that you have a choice about?

_____

_____

_____

4. Regarding work, if you could wave a magic wand, what or who would you remove from your life?

_____

_____

_____

Step 2 • More Whys and Wherefores

Describe briefly any of the following that apply to you and add a few thoughts on why each might be true.

1. Are there aspects of your career that no longer work for you?

_____

_____

_____

2.   Are you using strategies that have stopped getting results?

_____

_____

_____

3.   Is there anything that doesn't seem to matter as much as it did in the past?

_____

_____

_____

4.   Are there things that you no longer find satisfying?

_____

_____

_____

Note: Please resist the temptation to leap to the next step, the "therefore I should . . . (fix, change, do, etc.)." For now, the purpose of these questions is for you to begin to open the doors and clarify some of your current realities that you may or may not have looked at very deeply.

Step 3 • The PaperRoom Panel I—Goals

To complete step 3, you can begin with a blank sheet of paper, use the illustrated "Goals" shown on page 44, or download the "Goals" panel from *www.thepaperroom.com*. If you use a sheet of paper, you should fold it in half horizontally, and then in half again, so that when you unfold it, you have four sections, two at the top and two at the bottom.

Reenter the PaperRoom

As you turn, you see that the 36″ x 54″ paper wall panel is already set up with your name in the center of a cloud centered at the top of the paper. Next to it is a cloud with the date. There are three clouds in a line below that. The left cloud says "Long Term," the right says "Short Term," and in the middle is a cloud that says "Now!"

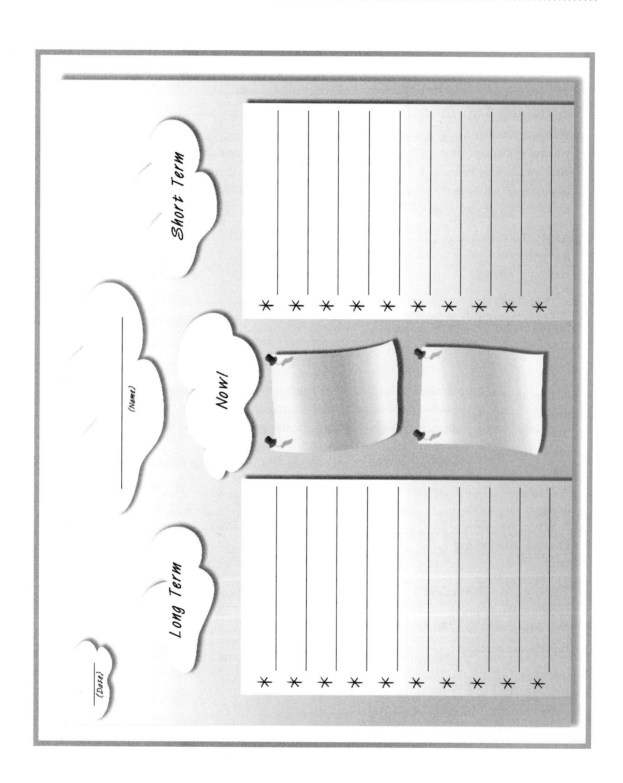

Long-Term Goals

The long-term goals we set in the PaperRoom are for twenty years in the future. If you are in your late twenties or thirties you will want to be thinking about how your life will look when you are embarking on your "second (or next) career," when you have some good solid experience under your belt and fewer immediate financial needs. If you are in your late forties or beyond, you will want to think about how you would like to see your life in your fourth quarter (seventy-five and older).

Although we are going to focus on your career throughout this book, when we set goals we are going to look at your whole life because, as far as I can tell, we take our whole selves to work. Having a fulfilling job is tied closely to having a fulfilling life. Because we will have many choices and opportunities as well as some constraints in the future that we couldn't know about now, the items you list as your long-term goals should reflect how you want to feel, or the qualities you want to have in your life at that age.

For instance, in the area of finances, you might want to say "comfortable," "stable," or "secure" (or all three) rather than give a dollar amount. We don't know what the dollar will be worth, but you do know how you want to feel about it financially. For your professional goals you might want to say "to be respected in my field" or "doing fulfilling work," because you cannot know exactly what the future will bring, but you know how you want to feel about your professional life. In the area of home, or homes, you might say, "have a house in the woods," and in saying that you actually have a whole picture of how your life and lifestyle will be. Then in twenty years when you happen to be living by the sea, you should be able to look and say, "Oh yes, this is my house in the woods." I grew up in California and always hoped someday I would be living in a comfortable Spanish-style house with a tiled roof. I had no idea I would be living in New England, and although I didn't plan it this way, it turns out that our wonderful eighteenth-century farmhouse feels just as I had imagined my Spanish-style home would.

The areas you want to look at and include in your long-term goals are health, finances, home, vocation, avocation, relationships, family, community, and spirituality. Remember, this is what you want, not necessarily what you think is possible. Below are some examples from two PaperRoom participants, both successful professionals.

Long-term goals of Philip (29):

Happily Married

2 kids

Working in a profession that makes a difference

In good shape

$$ comfortable

Rock climbing, snow boarding, etc.

Home in Boston area + another one somewhere

Long-term goals of Hope (46):

Cabin on a lake in Maine

Portfolio of income-generating businesses

Solid portfolio of investments

Healthy, loving personal life

Balanced life

Close group of friends and community

Be useful volunteering

Travel

Playing the piano professionally

Short-Term Goals

Short-term goals are targeted for the next twelve to eighteen months from now. These need to be clear, no-nonsense goals: how many, how much, and by when. The kinds of things you want to put on your short-term goals list are the things you need or want to get done yet have no current history of accomplishing, the things you have been putting off or not getting around to. Examples might include having that difficult conversation you have been avoiding, organizing your files, getting out the report that is overdue, bringing your résumé up to date, exercising three times a week, finding a new job, spending more time with your family, taking time just for yourself, and so on.

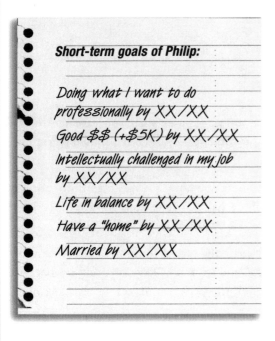

Short-term goals of Philip:

Doing what I want to do professionally by XX/XX

Good $$ (+$5K) by XX/XX

Intellectually challenged in my job by XX/XX

Life in balance by XX/XX

Have a "home" by XX/XX

Married by XX/XX

Short-term goals of Hope:

Decide about what I'm going to do professionally by XX/XX

Have a long-term strategy by XX/XX

Get published by XX/XX

Start doing more of what I like to do beginning XX/XX

Learn to play the flute beginning XX/XX

Create my future with Jack by XX/XX

Take care of my Mom beginning XX/XX

Generate 85K this year

Maintain a healthy lifestyle by XX/XX

Now! goals of Philip:

- Get unscrambled
- Be more confident
- Relax

Now! goals of Hope:

- Get unstuck
- Have clarity about how to express what I do professionally
- Focus!
- Lighten up! Have fun!

Goals for Now!

If you were in the PaperRoom, I would ask you what you would want when you leave here today if I could do magic. Your list would not need to be practical or possible, but it should reflect the core results you want from reading this book.

We've talked about choice points, how to recognize them and how they vary according to one's time of life. You now know about the Progress Path of Change, you've done an exercise exploring what stops you, and you've laid out some long-term and short-term goals.

Now we're going to talk about hidden beliefs and where they come from. You'll become more familiar with the beliefs I call your "Silent Partners," and learn how to recognize flags that tell you when they're taking over. In the next exercise, you will begin the process of revealing your Silent Partners.

CHAPTER THREE

Revealing the Invisible

Doing the PaperRoom has opened me to myself, shown me who I really am. I now see that all along through my career I thought I was an introvert. When people told me, "You're doing great," I didn't believe it. I wanted to avoid the lime-light but always seemed to end up there. Now I see myself for who I am. I actually thrive in the limelight. I'm a very good manager, a good leader. Before, beliefs I couldn't even see stopped me from giving myself credit for who I am. The PaperRoom flushed me out. — Casey

In this third of four
Scanning chapters you will:

- *Explore the origins of your hidden beliefs*
- *Learn how Silent Partners operate*
- *See the legacy of identity you've inherited*
- *Create a profile of your Silent Partners*

Your Hidden Beliefs

So what about those invisible gears in the Results System model you saw in chapter 1? "How do I discover or review something that is invisible?" you logically ask. Good question. We begin the PaperRoom at the root level of your experience, looking first for these invisible yet powerful gears turning in the background of your life, continually (for better or worse) influencing and filtering the choices you have, the actions you take, and the results you get.

This is how Bob discovered the invisible gears that had been running his life. He had a rich life, was successful in every way, yet found himself suddenly dissatisfied without understanding why.

THE ROLLER COASTER MAN AND THE CARDINAL

Bob enters the PaperRoom. He is a dynamic man in his mid-forties who is married, has three terrific teenage children, and has a self-designed job as a management consultant, making a handsome salary. He is known for being creative, innovative, and a fearless leader of change. But the old spark is gone. Work takes more out of him than it puts back. And he's suddenly getting a reputation for being insensitive.

Bob's capacity to remain afloat on the stormy seas of change is legendary. In fact, if things get too calm, he goes in and stirs them up again. It is no surprise that one of his favorite childhood memories is the joy of riding the roller coaster at Paragon Park in Hull, Massachusetts. As he recalls one day in particular, "It was the day after high school graduation, a day of celebrating a sense of freedom and achievement." So what did Bob do? He rode the roller coaster twenty-three times in a row!

Bob is a middle child who says he felt pretty invisible to his family, except for his Italian grandmother, who spoke no English. Bob was her favorite, in no small measure because he was the only one in the family who bothered to learn Italian. "I spent a lot of time with Nonni, listening to her stories of growing up in Italy in their little town of Terrasini. Nonni was certain I would grow up to be the priest in the family. Every noteworthy family in Italy has a priest in the family and ours would be no different." Bob's Nonni loved him unconditionally. She knew he was special. She recognized his ability to lead. She saw his heart.

Bob has consistently led successful efforts for substantive cultural change. But ironically, Bob himself has been changing; that special something his grandmother saw in him is beginning to emerge. "I find myself thinking more and more about giving to others; my kids are getting older, work is somewhat business-as-usual. I need to be pulled, to be challenged, to be somewhat uncomfortable. I know I'm looking for the next roller coaster event in my life."

After Bob's PaperRoom session, through a complicated set of circumstances demanding perseverance, he became a volunteer at a state prison. He chose to spend time with a group of "lifers" on a regular basis, to help them find value in their lives.

I felt a strong pull to go into the prisons and provide them with something. In spite of their crimes, these people are human beings who have taken a bad turn, and I felt it was my duty or calling to go to them. What I provide is someone to bounce things off and someone with a nonprison perspective, someone who cares. It feels very spiritual to go there. I sometimes feel like I am there doing God's work. I feel more alive, more challenged, more invigorated every time I leave those barbed wire gates.

This was the kind of charge Bob used to get from work.

When I discover a metaphor that captures the essence of someone's next appropriate developmental step, my client and I give it a name so that we can distinguish between old ways of seeing and dealing with situations versus new choices. Bob and I named his focus in the past the "Roller Coaster Man," and I suggested the new focus be named the "Priest." Bob, however, ego fully intact, preferred the term "Cardinal." Bob sees both the Roller Coaster Man and the Cardinal as parts of himself. The roller coaster represents the part of him that needs to be challenged, pulled out of his comfort zone and onto the edge, while the cardinal represents the side of him that wants to make a difference in other people's lives.

Bob's emerging feelings of dissatisfaction were letting him know that something was missing. He was doing things as he had done them in the past but not getting the same results— that is, the fact that he was "suddenly getting a reputation for being insensitive" was an indication that something either inside or outside of himself was changing or had changed and he needed to address it. As Bob matured and became more confi-

"Sometimes it takes years to really grasp what has happened to your life."

—**Wilma Rudolph, a disabled black woman in segregated Tennessee, and the first American woman to win three gold medals in the Olympics (1960)**

"My chiefest obstacles are within myself."

—**Rutherford B. Hayes, U.S. president**

dent, his need to explore doing things that were more deeply meaningful for him began to emerge. He was ready to explore doing things differently, but his Silent Partners were ruling the roost and causing him to repeat the patterns of the past at work. It wasn't until he started exploring outside the workplace that he could begin to experiment with new ways of behaving; and as he became more facile in doing and seeing things differently, he could gradually begin to add a new layer or two to his professional dimension.

Moving Ahead

The exercises in this chapter will help you begin the reflective process that Bob has already experienced. The process for Personal Inquiry 3 has two parts. In step 1 you will record some information about your parents and another important parental figure, if you had one. You'll be looking at what you thought about them as well as how you felt when you were around them.

In step 2 you will do another exercise, this time showing you how to use the information from step 1 to reveal your Silent Partners. When you reach the end of this chapter, you'll be tempted to think you've got your answers about what to do with this new information, but don't be seduced by your new insights. We've only just begun. Later you'll learn how to get the upper hand on this system so that you can run it and it won't run you. Hang in there. You'll see how this can work for you, too!

"Those who cannot remember the past are condemned to repeat it."
—George Santayana, philosopher

Accessing Your Silent Partners

You are now ready to examine your roots, but you're not going to dig into history and genealogy to create a family tree. Instead, you will dig into the things you may have learned earlier in life without knowing it. We'll continue with step 2 of this personal inquiry at the end of the chapter.

Step 1 • Your Family Legacy of Identity

Take an 8.5"x 11" piece of paper and title it "Family." Fold the page down, and then across, dividing it into four sections. Label the first section "Mother," the second "Father," and the third section with the name of another important adult who you were close to when you were growing up, if one comes to mind. Label the last section with your name (see sample on page 56). You can also go to *www.thepaperroom.com* and download panel 2.

The Third Adult

Identifying a possible third adult or other parental figure needs a bit more explaining so that you understand what we are looking for. First of all, it's fine if you don't have an important person who wasn't your parent. But if there is a third person you think might qualify, here is how you know for sure:

- You should ask yourself, "Did this person add an important positive dimension to my experience of myself that my parents couldn't or wouldn't provide?"

- Include a person who lived with you only if that person was an important, positive influence on your life, whether or not you loved that person.

- Clients occasionally tell me they had an older sibling who felt like a parent. If that is true for you, that person might qualify, but my experience is that regardless of his or her importance, when you understand the role your third person fulfills, you will see that your sibling would not be quite right.

- We are not talking about simply an ally here, although this person may be one. The importance of this person would be that you truly experienced him or her as another parent.

- We sometimes run across more than one person who seems right. Again, with very few exceptions, my experience is that there is only one who really fits the description. My suggestion is to pick the one who somehow gave you the deepest positive sense of self, rather than the one with whom you might have spent more time or had more fun.

Your Parents' Traits

List five to seven traits that reflect how you saw each of your parents (or third adult, if applicable) when you were growing up and still living at home.

In the PaperRoom, I use a different color marker to represent each person. This helps to distinguish the different connections later when you are working with the material in step 2. I print everything having to do with a particular person in his or her unique color, so you might want to do the same or use initials for each person, rather than colors, as I have in this book.

The words or phrases you use to describe each person should be in the present tense, as you would have said them when you were growing up. For instance, rather than writing, "Was always busy" you would write "Busy" or "Is busy." In the PaperRoom I say, "Pretend I just moved into the neighborhood and you took me into your confidence and wanted me to know exactly what your parents are like. I want to be able to see them through your eyes, warts and all."

Some of the things you want to look for are temperament, general likes and dislikes, talents, values, work or profession, and physical attributes if they were important to you at the time or important to your parent.

If you're having trouble jotting down notes, here are a few pointers:

- Use the words you might have used then. It is important to avoid using words or perspective from the wisdom of adulthood. It is also important to be brutally honest. The bad and the awful are as appropriate as the good, the wonderful, and the sublime. What is important is that you have said what you felt at that time, when you were growing up.

- If you saw your parents differently as you got older or circumstances changed, list those attributes as well, as long as those changes happened before you left high school.

Family

Other Important Person

Me

Mother

Father

- Stick to traits and descriptors you would say were true for the person and avoid slipping into how you thought he or she felt about you. You want to use adjectives, such as *talented, smart, unpredictable, angry, stressed, funny*, or name things that he or she loved (e.g., kids, tennis, being the center of attention) or disliked (e.g., sports, crowds, violent movies).

Your Traits

Pick a color (or initials) to represent yourself and use it when you answer questions about yourself on the "Family" panel.

Remember How You Felt Imagine yourself with each person separately. See if you can remember the personal traits you felt you had when you were around each person, or what you thought about yourself when you were with him or her. This is an unusual question most of us have not thought about. What we are looking for here is how you experienced yourself with each person. When you were around that person did you feel smart, stupid, competent, uncertain, funny, quiet, or what? For example, think about when you are with someone who thinks you are funny: *aren't* you funny with him or her? Or, when you are with someone that you know doesn't think much of your ideas, think about how difficult it is to have a creative thought around that person. Thinking of each person separately, list the attributes each of your parents might have ascribed to you and then list what your third person (if you listed one) might have said to describe you. If you are having difficulty, think about how they might have described you back then to someone who hadn't met you. What do you think they might have said? Or recall things they actually did say: "You always . . . ," "You're the one that . . . ," "I can always count on you for . . . . " Then try to remember how you felt, or how you felt about yourself, at that time.

Going Deeper When you have answered the questions for each of your three parental figures, go through the list again to note where you felt the same way with more than one person, or where you felt that others in the group felt the same way about you.

For instance, if your mom and dad and the third person all thought you were funny, to the left of the word "Funny" you might place three colored stars (a different color for each person) or perhaps three sets of initials, or however you were doing your list. If, on the other hand, only two people thought you were smart, just those two people would be noted beside "Smart." If you felt shy with your third person but didn't feel shy with either of your parents, "Shy" would have just one indication beside it. The following suggestions may help you complete this step:

- If you don't know what that person thought, put down "Don't know."

- As you think about each person separately, you may find that the person you are working on held the same opinion of you as the previous person did. When that happens, you can simply put the colored symbol or initials of the person you are working on next to the previous occurrence of the opinion phrase. You don't need to write the opinion phrase twice.

Now look at the following information regarding family, which will help you interpret what you've just written.

Some Information About Family: Early Learnings

As you may have guessed, the first place we learned our perceptions, assumptions, and habits was in our family. We may have simply been told that something was true—"Money is good, but too much money is bad"—and never really questioned it or found out exactly what it meant. After all, our parents were the experts, weren't they? We learned by seeing, hearing, being told, and taking (or not taking) action, and by deciding on something based on the result we got. Let's say, for instance, that when you were a kid you swiped a cookie and you got caught. At that point, you would have decided one of two things: not to steal cookies in the future, or to be more stealthy the next time.

And so, we continue to collect information, learning things, making decisions, and getting to know the world we live in. When a situation pops up that feels like a previous one, we've already done the homework, so we automatically do what we found worked in the past. The problem with that is we don't also have an opportunity to review all this clutter. We just move the new information in and shove the old thought back a little further. Without any critical review process, we continue to gather information or truths about our world randomly, even though they may conceivably conflict with one another.

For instance, let's say you're feeling stuck in your job, feeling like a worker bee when you really want management to take you more seriously. Up to now, you've taken pride in the way you hunker down and get the job done. You've been praised for your hard work ever since you were a kid. But now you're ready for something more. You want your boss to see you as "management material." So what do you do? You work harder to get even more done to make sure you get recognized. But does this really make sense? If your good work so far has not led others to think you are management material, why would revving up to do even more of the same get you a different result? If you want to be more visible to "the powers that be," how about starting to attend the weekly departmental meetings?

Can you think of an example like this in your own life?

_____

_____

_____

_____

In just such a way we continue to build our store of paradoxes throughout our life. If we don't periodically review our old assumptions and check them against the facts or current evidence, we go with what we have always done. It would be like continuing to have that nice Snickers bar for an afternoon snack when we say we are determined to lose weight. We end up with lives of short-range satisfaction but suffer long-range costs.

Step 2 • Revealing Your Silent Partners

Now it's time for an exercise designed to give you access to some of your earliest perceptions, habits, and expectations. You can then consider whether these Silent Partners are good for you, if they support the kinds of results you want in your career and life now or if they have been holding you back. The point here is to discover and learn. It is too early in the process to draw any final conclusions or to do anything about your discoveries. You will be looking at this information again later in the book, and it's important not to shortcut the process if you want fundamental and lasting results.

Exercise Setup

You are now going to use the list you just made in step 1 to look a little more deeply into what those descriptions might mean in your life. Here is a simple example of how this might work. Let's say that when you were growing up in your family, your mom always served applesauce with pork chops, so now when you go to the market to buy pork chops you say to yourself,

"Hmmm, I need to buy applesauce." Applesauce automatically goes with pork chops. You don't say, "No problem, I have *cranberry* sauce." But why not? Cranberry sauce would actually taste pretty good with pork chops. (Nevermind the fact that *obviously* cranberry sauce is for Thanksgiving turkey dinner!) What you will be doing in this next exercise is identifying "the applesauce," the automatic thoughts you have about what naturally goes with each of the traits you have listed in step 1.

First let's develop a more workable metaphor than pork chops and applesauce. Imagine that the attributes or traits that you attributed to each person in step 1 were at the tip of an iceberg, and that the accompanying Silent Partners were the information "below the water line," the perceptions, beliefs, habits, expectations, and assumptions that accompany the attribute for that person. See figure 3, "Family Influence."

For instance, if the first trait you listed for your mother was "organized," picture that as the tip of the iceberg. Not everyone is organized in the same way, nor is there a universal "right" way to be organized. The remaining and largest part of the iceberg, stretching deep below the surface, would be made up of your mother's Silent Partners influencing her concept of being organized. These would be her beliefs about being organized, her mental and physical habits regarding what she does about being organized, and the results she expects when she has carried out these actions. You would now want to jot down next to this trait some of these characteristics.

You could learn much from this example. You could have learned from your observation of what your mother did or didn't do and the results that produced. Also, because this was so clear to you, you could have understood or recognized what was *not* "organized behavior." Additionally, you could have learned your mother's beliefs about, expectations of, and habits in being organized. It is these "below the water line" learnings that can cause the most mischief. They are generally as invisible and automatic for us as they were for our parent, and we are just as likely never to consider whether or not this way of doing or seeing things is useful for us.

Completing the Exercise

You can complete this exercise any way you are most comfortable. You can tack your sheet up somewhere, make notes on your "Family" page, make comments using stickies, write your observations in a separate notebook, tape-record your comments and discoveries to listen to and review at a later date, or just do the work in your head. Any or all of the above will work.

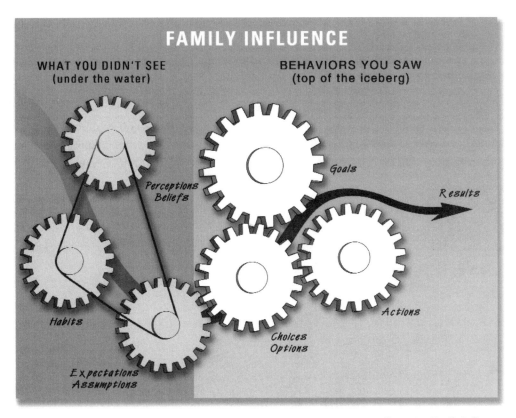

Figure 3 • Family Influence

As you identify and elaborate on the traits you have on your list for each person, you will want to notice how, or if, they also apply to you, and write that down. Back to Mom. If your mother was organized, are you organized in the same way? Do you have the same feelings, opinions, and "shoulds" about being organized? Most likely your mother would have become upset if any of her organizing methods were unavailable or unfeasible or if the results were different than she expected. In relation to the facets of this trait of your mother's, what is true for you? Notice any thoughts you have in your life about the trait and if that thinking helps you get things done or gets in your way.

Now, referring to the list of attributes you have given to each parent (and your third person), write down your observations about each one. Stick with this process as long as you are interested, and when or if it starts to get tedious, put it away and come back to it at a later time. The idea of this exercise is to discover some of your Silent Partners by starting outside yourself and looking at your family to get a hint of what beliefs, habits, expectations, and/or assumptions may have been guiding you without your knowledge.

Once you understand the concept, it is not necessary to complete all the work with each attribute before moving on. If, however, you feel that it's likely that you will not come back to complete it, don't go on until you finish. The process will still work if you don't, but obviously your discoveries and results will be less meaningful and will lack depth. It's up to you.

Working on the exercises in this chapter, you have begun to unearth some insights into what's been making you tick. We'll use this material you've generated again, as we continue to work through the process chapter by chapter. We have only just begun. The "you" portion of this panel will be completed in a later chapter after you have learned some new concepts and have learned the value and uses of this information.

CHAPTER FOUR

Hidden Influences

I'd always made career choices the same as my peers, always going for the bigger title and greater prestige. Right after doing the PaperRoom, I was offered a job in New York, in senior management, but then I knew status wasn't what was important to me. I've always worked with senior executives, and I think a lot of people get there because of politics and power, not necessarily because they did the right thing. This time I wanted to be true to my values, so I thought, "If I move up, I give up some of my integrity and individuality." — Jeff

In this fourth of four
    Scanning chapters you will:

• Explore the hidden influences in your work

• See how our environments "live us"

• Discover your invisible norms

• Map out the patterns in your work history

The Hidden Influences in Your Work

made a most interesting observation in one of my entrepre-
neurial ventures. I had a corporate catering business, bringing breakfast and lunch carts to organizations in downtown
Boston. The first few times I tended to a new client, I went with
the carts to make sure everything was set up properly. I noticed
a really interesting thing as I went from business to business:
even though many of the law offices or stock brokerage businesses did the same sort of work, opening the door to each company was as different as changing channels on the television. It
wasn't just that the décor was different; the people actually
seemed very different as well. Some offices were formal and
quiet; some had a lot of energy. Some were open, while others
had all the doors closed. People dressed differently and acted

differently as well. But like a play or a television program, in each business it all seemed to go together; overall, each had its own unique personality. Did the hiring people in each business hire only people like themselves, or was there something about each environment that brought out specific things in people? Probably some of each.

In the last chapter we opened the door to the Silent Partners that you first acquired in your childhood. We saw that as our life progressed and our experience expanded, each time we learned a new skill, mastered a new activity, or visited a new place—as life unfolded in its myriad ways—we added knowledge into our automatic system for handling things. As we moved through life, successes or less positive results influenced how we saw our options, how we made our choices, and how we established our goals. In addition to all of that, we were and are daily heavily influenced by something less obvious—the world around us.

A Story of Changes

Have you ever made a move—to another job or another town or another part of the country—and all of a sudden felt yourself to be out of your element? Only at such times do we become poignantly aware of how we take for granted the norms of our day-to-day life. In 1965, I moved to New England from Los Angeles, newly married and ready to start a new life. That first year was filled with surprises, both wonderful and not so great. I had moved to a whole new world that seemed to have more things different than the same. The differences were best captured in my first League of Women Voters meeting.

Norman and I had moved to an apartment, had bought some furniture, and were settling in. My job was in another town, and I decided that if I was ever going to know anyone where we lived, I needed to join something. It was winter, so no

"The way to be new is to be yourself. . . . The only you you have. Keep it clear as you can."
—Georgia O'Keeffe, artist

Have you noticed minicultures within your communities?

_____

_____

_____

_____

"We give up three-fourths of ourselves to be like other people."
—Arthur Schopenhauer, philosopher

garden club—I didn't have a garden anyhow. No PTA—no kids yet. When I saw the notice for the League of Women Voters meeting it seemed to fit the bill—I did vote. The meeting was in the evening, and they apparently met quarterly, a comfortable start for me, I thought.

As I entered Grange Hall with the other women and was removing my coat and hat and stamping the snow from my boots with the others, I couldn't help thinking that this was like a Currier and Ives tableau brought to life. The cold metal fold-up seats scraped the wooden floor, creaking and ticking as we took our seats.

The meeting was brought to order by a substantial woman in tweed. She read the minutes of the last meeting and presented the evening's agenda, which would begin with a discussion of the annual dues. It seemed there had been a suggestion that the price for attending the quarterly meetings be raised, from $1.00 to $1.25, bringing the annual total to $5.00. Things proceeded relatively predictably and politely as questions were raised about the necessity of this action, where the needed money might be raised and so forth. Then about ten minutes into the discussion a woman who had not been called on virtually burst out of her seat, bellowing that this was absolutely outrageous.

"What about the poor people?" she said. Did we realize we were thoughtlessly becoming "discriminatory, exclusive, and elitist?" It took me a minute to realize that her angry tirade was about the proposed twenty-five-cent increase, and that she was by no means alone in her concern. Much to my amazement, the room raged on for the remainder of the meeting. Here I was, straight out of L.A., movieland's land of the grand gesture, witnessing the heated discussion of the pros and cons of upping the annual dues by a dollar. Where I came from, projecting the image of conspicuous largesse was a desired given, regardless of one's finances. And I thought I would have felt out of place at the garden club!

How Our Environments Live Us

The women of L.A. and the women of New England, though similar in means, lived in a world of very different social norms. The offices I visited likewise varied dramatically in their environmental tone and character. And the understanding I've developed over the years to explain this phenomenon is that we do not so much create our environments or live in our environments as our environments "live" us.

Our Silent Partners not only help us filter out choices based on the things we have successfully done in the past; they also help us to behave unconsciously in concert with our environment. These norms of working and living become so much a part of the fabric of our lives that we rarely step back to notice them. Often we cannot see them unless we have temporarily or permanently moved away. Then we are able to "see the forest for the trees." Indeed, it would be difficult for us to avoid going along with "the way things are," or even to know that it is something we do in which we have a choice.

How Your Environments Live You

External norms work in the same way as our other Silent Partners, ensuring that we comply by using the same three lines of defense: not noticing, feeling uncomfortable about doing things differently, and finding good reasons why we shouldn't bother. In the next exercise you will begin discovering these invisible influences in your life. You'll see how you have (or have not) woven them into your perception of which opportunities are (or aren't) available to you. It will give you a deeper under-

Have you ever felt suddenly out of your element? When?

_____

_____

_____

_____

_____

standing of what to look for, what to avoid, and what you might be able to change to make a difficult situation better. These discoveries may also shed some light on the behaviors of those around you and your reactions to them. Personal Inquiry 4 is designed to reveal your patterns of predictable behavior. In this exercise you are going to discover some of your predictable patterns in regard to:

- The environments you are attracted to

- Your behavior around different personalities

- The depth of your experience

- Your established method for successful personal change management

- Identifying the professional environments that best serve you

- Navigating your career

Patterns

This is the only exercise in the book that actually gives you access to your patterns and provides you with the foundation you will need to gain the most value from Personal Inquiry 5. This expanded awareness will enable you to better manage the things you can leverage and to change the patterns that don't serve you. This process has two parts. In step 1 you will be asked to list information about each of your jobs. In step 2 you will learn what the information means so that you can begin to recognize your Silent Partners.

Step 1 • Job Information

Take out an 8.5" x 11" piece of paper, divide it into six columns, and title the sheet "Patterns." Then label your columns with these six headings: "Where?" "Who?" "What?" "How?" "How Long?" and "Why Left?" Or you can use the "Patterns" panel on page 70 or download and use the "Patterns" panel template at *www.thepaperroom.com.*

On this sheet, list all your jobs beginning with your first babysitting job or the equivalent. This is not your résumé. You should also include any volunteer positions you felt were actual jobs, for example, president of the Glee Club. This list should be in chronological order, but don't fret: a slight mistake will not change your results as long as things are generally in the right order.

Because you are putting down all your jobs, including your summer or school-related jobs and any significant volunteering, you may have a long list. And if you have been active in your community, it may be considerably longer. This is not a bad thing. Many of us have some embarrassment about aspects of our work history. It's normal to find it easier to see what is wrong than what is right. This is not a time for judging what you've done, but rather a time to observe and learn about your patterns. You are going to discover strengths, richness, and some interesting information you didn't even know was there.

Starting with your first job, answer each of the following questions before going on to the next job, and continue in this way until you have completed your job history.

- **Where?** In this column name the businesses or organizations you worked for or, if you don't recall the name, fill in the kind of place it was: food shop, factory, etc. (if you started with babysitting, you would list the place as "neighborhood").

- **Who?** This column is for the name of your boss. If you were your own boss, write "me." If you cannot remember the person's name just put "M" for man, or "W" for woman. If you can't remember at all, "?" is also fine.

- **What?** In this column list your job titles or descriptions.

- **How?** How did you get your job? For instance: "advertisement," "head hunter," "agency," "I asked," "they asked me," "I was promoted," "I networked" (including any job you got through friends, family, or any traditional networking process).

- **How Long?** How long did you stay in that job before you left the organization or took a new position in the same organization? When you have held more than one position in the same organization, or had the same boss for successive jobs, it is not necessary to list the name of the business or boss again.

- **Why Left?** Why did you leave that job, position, or organization? "Let go," "fired," and/or "hated it" are all possibilities, as are more money, moved, graduated, etc.

Be sure to finish this exercise before going on to step 2.

Step 2 • Seeing Your Work Patterns

This can be a most interesting part of the exercise because it is the one we *think* we know the most about. It can also be the most difficult because, within your familiar work history, I am going to ask you to find some new information and to identify what of that new information is good. The more you know now about the patterns that brought you this far, the better you will be at avoiding mistakes, learning what you need to learn, and leveraging your knowledge in the future.

Normally when we look at a resume or a work history, we look at how, or if, one job somehow led to the other in a linear fashion. But when you read your "Patterns" page, you will be looking *down* each column, rather than across, looking at each job. To make it easier, draw a line vertically separating the columns, if you haven't already. In the PaperRoom, I put the last two columns, "How Long?" and "Why Left?," together. That makes it possible to recognize more easily the short-lived nature of your first jobs, as they were likely summer jobs or related to the school year in some way.

In this process, you can discover where and when you have followed patterns learned from your family, and where and when you have started to develop some of your own. Also, as you work with this section, you will have an opportunity to see if you need any additions to your long-range and short-range goals or adjustments to any of the goals you currently have on your list.

Patterns of behavior are habits that are difficult to change. Whenever possible, it is useful to leverage or use them to your best advantage rather than try to replace or change them. Better to find the job that fits you than to try to fit yourself to the job. Too much "trying to fit in" robs us of much of our creativity and takes precious time and energy away from our work.

Once again, you can do this exercise in any way that works for you. I suggest you do one column at a time with breaks (hours, days) in between. The time when you are not directly working with your material will be an opportunity for you to process the information a bit more, which can lead to more insights. Also, giving yourself a break will help you avoid "process burnout."

Looking at the Results

Now you can begin to examine the results of your exploration into your past work experiences. Using questions following the descriptions for each heading can help you discover your hidden influences. Start with the first column and work your way down.

Where? A study of your notes in the "Where?" column reveals some interesting facts:

- The kinds of environments you're drawn to

- The kinds of organizations that hire you or see you as being valuable

- The kinds of organizations you naturally choose

Try looking beyond what the business does to what kind of an environment it is, how it looks, what sort of folks work there. Notice the path and pattern of your work and how these have evolved over time. In the beginning, the kind of professional work you did is often somehow related to your family. As you progress, work becomes a better reflection of your own desires and established skills.

Patterns function as filters so that our choices are guided by what we are used to. This is not necessarily a bad thing, but it may be limiting your ability to understand why your current job doesn't feel like a "right fit" or to expand your search for other opportunities that you may not have considered. For instance, if you have always worked in smaller organizations, you might not consider a large corporate environment, thinking ("knowing") it is not for you. You wouldn't know, for instance, that although corporate cultures may look impersonal from the outside, in fact working in a department can often feel like being part of a small business. You might need to dress differently, or learn some new acronyms or some new business norms, but those things are not insurmountable, and you might like the change. The same, of course, goes for the reverse. What other business could use your services that you have not considered?

Compare the organizations you have worked in with the job histories and attitudes/beliefs of your parents.

- Is there anything to discover there?

- Are you automatically repeating or rebelling against a pattern you observed/learned from them?

- If so, are there ways in which they might have consciously or unconsciously influenced your decisions?

- Looking back at your "Goals" panel, is there anything to discover or learn there?

- Do you see any changes or new opportunities you need to explore to reach your long-term goals?

- Do you see any connections between your short-term goals and your childhood or your parents?

- Has something you learned to resist or avoid become a habit? If so, consider looking at this assumption again to make sure your reasoning is still relevant.

Who? Your notes in the "Who?" column will give you clues about the kinds of personalities you are comfortable working with and those you are not, as well as insights into how different personalities have influenced your perception of the job and your quality of work. As you think about each individual on your list, reflect on these questions:

- Can you see where that person shared or did not share your values and what that might have contributed to your perception of the job?

- Regardless of your feelings about that person, what result did you produce under his or her supervision style?

- Do you see any connection between your reactions to that person and your reactions to your family (or third person)?

- If so, does this insight give you any reason to change anything on your "Goals" list?

What? The third column should reflect the depth of skills and knowledge acquired in your years of work. Looking at our work experience in linear blocks of time, we can overlook the breadth and depth of what we know.

- What have you done in the past ten days that you first learned about in your first job?

- Was it something to do with your understanding or expectations of the situation or people or of how the job should get done? (We draw from all our experience, always. This is one of the advantages of our Silent Partners: we don't need to learn the same thing over and over again.)

- Has one job or endeavor led to another, and why did you make the job choices you did along the way?

- Have you used the knowledge of your past as you moved forward? How?

- Have you made any decisions because of past job experiences that warrant reevaluating?

How? This column reveals the skills you have for getting new work and moving on in your career. Each client I've seen finds most of his or her jobs in a similar way, whether it's through ads, networking, promotions, or some other avenue. This is not by accident; this is a skill. You don't have to know how you do it or why it works; you just need to know that it works for you. Always leverage this skill for your best results in moving forward. You can certainly try other methods, but most likely the way you have found your jobs in the past will be the way you get most of your new ones in the future. There is one note of caution here. If historically you didn't get the jobs you wanted, obviously there is something you need to learn or change before going on to your next job interview. You will read about how to change your patterns in chapter 8, so for now just stay with your observation. There will be more to discover before you're finished.

How Long? The length of time you stayed on a job can highlight your need for change and/or reflect what was going on in your life at that point in time.

- Is there a time pattern that emerges for your staying in a certain location or doing a particular kind of work before you need to learn something new?

- As you review the jobs you liked and those you didn't, can you find any consistency or themes there?

- Which opinions were reflections of your family's values or how you felt you were seen as a child? What did you learn about yourself that could be useful?

The jobs you liked the best or in which you stayed the longest are likely to be the jobs that most closely fulfilled your needs and values. Your specific need to feel great about your work and the conditions you value are the same, regardless of your age or job history. You will learn much more about this in chapter 6. As you have probably already realized, the richness of each of these panels is ultimately in how it relates to the others.

Why Left? The "Why Left?" column is interesting because it reveals how you have given yourself permission to move on in the past.

- What may have been "decided" by outside factors—marriage, school, moving, etc.—versus personal decisions regarding dissatisfaction with the job?

- Are there any patterns?

- Does this list tell you anything about your current situation?

- Are you following any patterns set by your family of origin or their expectations of you that are not consistent with your own needs and values?

- Does this column illuminate or change anything on your "Goals" list?

- Are there conditions or circumstances you become more aware of when it is time to move on? Like what?

Some people decide to move on by getting fired. For this exercise, assume you had something to do with it if you were fired or let go. After all, we all know people who do not do their jobs well but never seem to get fired, and we know others who apparently do very good work but can't seem to hold on to a job. We can always imagine uncomplimentary reasons why those who don't do well are kept on. If you were let go:

- Why did they let you go?

- What was going on there that you felt wasn't right?

- What didn't meet your standards?

- What caused the job in some way to be unfulfilling?

In this chapter we checked out the hidden influences in your work and saw how our environments live us. You've learned about your Silent Partners and then mapped out the patterns in your work history.

In part 2 we will talk about the powerful impact "housecleaning" can have on maintaining forward motion. We'll also talk about the greater amount of time that's available to you now compared to in the past. Then you can try a little housecleaning of your own.

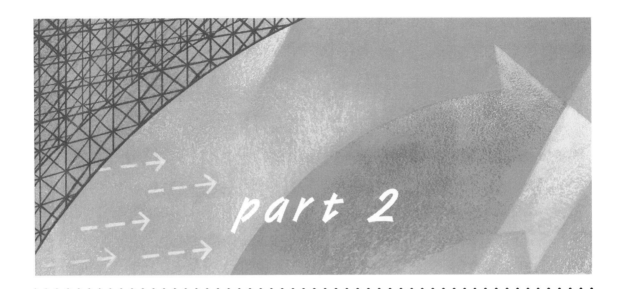

part 2

FOCUS

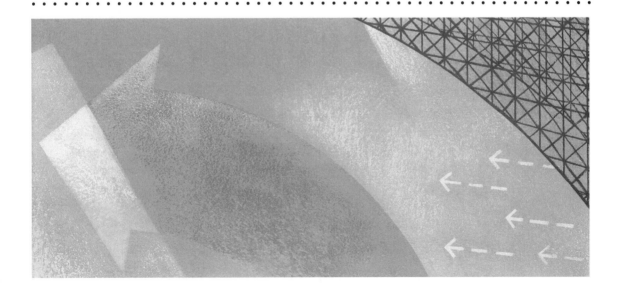

CHAPTER FIVE

Housecleaning

Now, as I go along making choices, I'm more conscious about satisfying my needs. I ask myself, "Can I live without the things that are missing from this job?" Before I wasn't conscious; I couldn't judge. Now I know what won't work. And I've gotten rid of all the old ideas in my head and things in my home that don't work for me either. I've really cleaned up my act. I'm so much more refined in my thinking about what I need. If a situation doesn't have what I need, there's no reason to go there. If something isn't going to support me, I get rid of it. — Sonja

In this first of two
Focus chapters you will:

● *Learn about the power of housecleaning*

● *Explore the Life Domains for your quarter of life*

● *Distinguish your life quarter purpose*

● *Begin your own housecleaning in your work and life*

Creating the Space for Change

It is said that nature abhors a vacuum and will quickly fill every one. When it comes to facilitating change or doing things differently, this is absolutely true. When we literally or figuratively "clear the space," change happens—something new fills the empty space. Making room for change is the first task on which to focus. When I am working with people in the PaperRoom who are making major professional changes and feel that things are not moving fast enough, I tell them to start cleaning—their desk, their files, their bookcases, the trunk of their car, whatever they can think of.

The Sign Maker

In the early years of my business, when I was working primarily as a consultant for change, I worked with many small "mom and pop" businesses that wanted or needed to become more profitable. One of my clients was Chuck. For years he had worked in a sign-making shop with his father. After his father retired, Chuck was able to "finally join the twenty-first century" by introducing then-new computerized sign-making equipment into his business. In two years he grew the business from one to eight employees. The shop was making many more signs than Chuck's dad ever thought possible, but even though the revenue was up, cash flow was always a problem, and the cost of doing business was extremely high.

When I went to see Chuck's operation, it was easy to see why he had difficulty making the business profitable. He had slick new technology, but there was no system or standard for doing anything. The standards and the system were left up to the individual making the sign. Chuck, of course, had learned the sign-making business from his father, who had always worked alone. When Chuck came in they had worked together, each using whatever space was available. Now the business was eight men making signs in any clear spot they could find. Interestingly, I noticed that the employees mirrored their environment. They rolled in any time they felt like it to get their signs finished, sometimes still disheveled from the night before.

We set out to "clean house" and began creating a business that was organized; we set standards and procedures for producing the signs and established consistent pricing, including reliable production time and cost estimates. Predictably, when Chuck started making new demands and required his workers to help design a new method of producing the signs, most of them weren't pleased. In fact, the only difference between how

"The wisdom of life consists in the elimination of nonessentials."

—Lin Yutang, philosopher

this news went over and the *Caine* mutiny was that this was on dry land. Doing old things in a new way can be no fun, regardless of how good the new idea is.

After a few months, only two of Chuck's original staff members were still with him. However, what was happening was very interesting. The more old, broken, and damaged material Chuck threw out, the more he cleaned, the more organized he became, the more business and profitability increased, without any additional advertising. Stranger yet, without anyone saying anything, the two remaining employees started coming in on time and were even combing their hair and tucking in their shirts. The new people coming to interview were people interested in working with a new technology and excited to have a hand in making it successful. Before the year was out, Chuck was doing twice the business at a greater profit than the business had yet known, and all he had done was clean house and get organized. Don't believe me? Try it yourself! Think of the mess in your work or living space that looks like your biggest obstacle to progress. Clean it up and notice what happens.

The Environmental Link to Your Silent Partners

Cleaning up and organizing seems to start things moving, and although it might seem your result is "magical," if you have been paying attention in the previous chapters, it all begins to make sense. When you change the physical environment, you are changing the cues your Silent Partners receive. This, of course, is what happened to the employees at Chuck's sign shop. The external cues—neatness, order, a system for doing things—not only attracted new employees who were comfortable with that kind of environment, but also shifted the signals the remaining employees received and thereby changed their behavior.

Which messes look like your biggest obstacles to progress?

_____

_____

_____

_____

If you go a step further along this path and begin to understand more broadly your old perceptions about your world and the opportunities available to you, you can choose which perceptions and habits serve you and which do not. We do this unconsciously all the time when we begin to feel differently about a situation, begin to work with new people, or go from one job to the next. We are very much like the employees who remained at the sign shop, who changed because *something* told them that their old behavior would not be acceptable in the new environment. The difference now is that we can make these changes consciously, by free choice.

Chapters 1 through 4 were about giving you the tools to expand your awareness about your Silent Partners, your internal systems. We started unearthing the hidden beliefs and the cultural influences that narrow your perceptions and so limit your ability to see clearly what's possible in the present. Chapters 5 and 6 are about putting your house in order to make room for the new challenges you have set for yourself. The sign shop could not stretch into a new level of business until Chuck became much more keenly aware of what was there—the good, the bad, and the awful. Only then could he remove what once was useful but was now cluttering the space, fix what was broken, buy what was needed, and design a system that supported the kinds of results he was seeking. This housecleaning included everything the business touched—the physical space, the materials, the bookkeeping, how employees were treated, everything.

Life Domains

Although we focus on things separately, our life is all of a piece, and we really cannot address something in one area without considering the whole. In the same way that Chuck the sign maker needed to review and refine everything in his business,

What areas have you focused on up to now?

_____

_____

_____

_____

_____

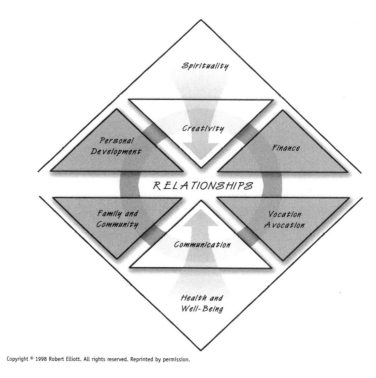

Figure 4 • Life Domains

you will need to evaluate all the parts of your life if you truly want a satisfying career. To do less would take you only partway to your goal.

Bob Elliott is a management consultant and the creator of "Elliott's Life Domains" model. His model could be a whole book in itself, but we are going to use it here as a reminder that all the aspects of our life are connected through relationship, creativity, and communication, and we really cannot address something in one area without considering the whole.

As you look at this model in figure 4, begin to notice the possible connections between the various domains and how each influences your quality of life. Also notice that although all domains are always somehow present, different areas of our life sometimes need more attention than others. The important thing is to notice what you are choosing to focus on and what you are not, and why that is important to you at this time. We will work with this model later in the chapter and will use it again in chapter 10.

The Space in Time

As long as we are on this quest to see what we aren't seeing, let's look at the issue of time. Assisting us in our quest to live life fully is a dramatic difference between the world we live in and the one our parents lived in when they were our age. We have more time, not less. Lots more time. We are healthier and more vigorous in our later years than previous generations were. We have a far longer life expectancy, in fact about twice as long as a century ago. In 1900 life expectancy in the United States was forty-three. But notice! We are still organizing our time as if we had only fifty healthy, vigorous years. *Married in our twenties, children in our twenties and thirties, career peaks at forty, retirement at sixty-five* is the general expectation. Retirement at sixty-five? We certainly might be ready for a different professional focus. We might be very ready to prioritize our time differently. But nothing but golf and puttering around the mall for twenty-five to thirty years—are you serious? Social Security was introduced in 1935 when life expectancy was sixty-three. It was intended to provide income for only a small percentage of our population. We don't need to jam all that is important about life into the first twenty or thirty years of adulthood and then coast to our inevitable demise. We don't need to do everything all at once.

Second-Quarter Focus

As we see that we have more time, we also realize that we have a different focus in each stage of our life. Working with clients in the PaperRoom, I began to notice that people in the earlier part

"Always be a work in progress."

—Tim DuBois, musician

Q2: Adult (25–50)

Theme: Creation and stability
Purpose: Providing for ourselves and future generations
Job: Building the future

What are, or were, your Q2 issues and concerns?

_____

_____

_____

_____

Q3: Mentor (50–75)

Theme: Contribution & community

Purpose: Authenticity

Job: Fulfilling who we know ourselves to be

of their career life are looking for very different things than they are later in their career.

When we are younger, we are trying to find the right profession or the right job to establish ourselves in a career that is the right "fit," has the potential to afford us the kind of life we want to live, and provides financially for our needs. This is not only a "money thing," however. We are being pulled to *become* something, to achieve a life that's aligned with our ideals and hopes. The second quarter is about learning, experimenting, and providing for ourselves and others. Since we don't yet have a full life of experiences, our approach is necessarily outwardly focused—we want to be a designer or a nurse, work with computers, work with people. Like choosing clothes off a rack, we try on the careers or work paths that appeal to us for both practical and emotional reasons. We are *becoming*. The challenge is to fulfill our responsibilities, to establish our place in society at the same time that we build a stable structure to support ourselves and possibly raise a family. In the PaperRoom, long-term professional goals for people in Q2 are often something like "working in a job I love" or "being recognized in my field."

Is this true for you? Or, if you are beyond this stage, was it true for you?

Third-Quarter Focus

The good news is that regardless of what we did in the first part of our adult life, it is useful for the second. I like to say that life up to fifty is the exact right homework for what we are really going to do "when we grow up." People in their late forties to mid-fifties are generally looking for something quite different from what they sought when they were younger, even though they may be describing it the same way—a job that fits, a job that lets them balance their life in a manner that feels fulfilling.

And herein lies the difficulty we often have professionally: when we hit our middle years, we are not exactly looking to become something so much as we are looking to fulfill some deeper need. For instance, making money becomes less important than "making a difference." "Contribution" and "community" are the words that often appear as people's PaperRoom long-term goals. We don't have the same responsibilities to our children or, at some point, to our parents. In a very different way and from a completely different perspective, we once again have more freedom to be creative about what we do with our professional life and what kinds of challenges we want to take on. In our third quarter, both the challenge and the opportunity are to take the career we've built and align it with and incorporate it into what is important to us now, to make our life finally a full expression of who we now know ourselves to be.

No "Up" to Get To

I believe that much of our current frustration comes from not appreciating and taking advantage of our expanded opportunities. A longer life expectancy means that we now have time to get all the richness each life quarter has to offer, yet rarely do we stop and reevaluate our expectations for ourselves given these new realities. One of the powerfully persistent concepts that keeps us from fully appreciating our evolving adulthood is embedded in our language. It is the whole notion of "growing up." You must recognize that there is no "up" to get to—we just continue to evolve and grow.

Regardless of which life quarter we are in, the addition of more healthy years of life means that the way we have thought about our "working years" can, and probably should, change. But it is going to take some creativity, innovation, and willingness to experiment to find a better way.

What are your Q3 issues and concerns?

_____

_____

_____

_____

_____

"Don't go through life, GROW through life."

—Eric Butterworth, minister and author

Housecleaning in Q2 and Q3

We naturally expect to do some reorganizing and house-cleaning when things change, especially at the end of something—a project, a job, or a change of bosses. Sometimes change is brought on by the seasons, the economy, or a move to a new location. While it seems I have always known this, until recently I hadn't been so keenly aware that different life stages require that we do some housecleaning as well. Let's now take a closer look at the characteristics of the second and third quarters of life that we introduced in chapter 2.

Q2 (ages 25–50): The general focus is on building and sta-bilizing your career to balance and ensure the qualities and experiences you want in your life now, and to ensure the accomplishments and results you want as you move into Q3. The policies, procedures, people, places (home and work), and "equipment" needed to support those goals need to be put into place. The many components of this stage of life necessitate regular housecleaning to create and maintain balance.

Q3 (ages 50–75): Accumulated experience makes it possible to evaluate your career from a different perspective. For many it's time for a housecleaning to "make the space" to fully realize the remarkable professional and personal opportunities of Q3.

Whatever your time of life, if what you are after is to live life to its maximum, I recommend that you do the "housecleaning" exercise at the end of this chapter on a regular basis. For some, this means yearly; for others, every three or four years. As the seasons of your life change, some additional major houseclean-ing is important as well.

Your Housecleaning

"Housecleaning" is the first of the two focusing exercises in part 2, "Focus." Regardless of what you have discovered or accomplished since you began reading this book, this is where "the rubber meets the road." Way back in chapter 1, we began to explore your Silent Partners, those invisible perceptions, beliefs, habits, expectations, and assumptions that are the filters through which you have been seeing your goal options and choices. We now move from the invisible to the visible. The work you have done so far has given you the background to apply your new career/life perspective.

You've paved the way for using the navigational tools that will make many more things possible. The goal in chapters 5 through 8 is to learn what these tools are and what you can accomplish with them, and to recognize when and how to use them.

You should start, as Chuck the sign maker did, with the most simple, obvious, and basic step: cleaning up your physical environment. Don't underestimate the impact this can have on your career and the rest of your life. And the good news is that you will begin reaping the benefits as soon as you start.

Housecleaning Exercise

In this exercise we focus on three areas: physical space, your Life Domains, and your short- and long-term goals. Notice how each one requires a unique sort of housecleaning.

Area One: Physical Space

Set aside some time to clean out your work space, half an hour each day, two hours a week, whatever you can comfortably fit into your schedule and complete, given your history of follow-through. As you begin to sort and organize, ask yourself the following questions about each item there:

- Do I need this? Does this support me in at least one of my priorities?

- Would my life be diminished in any way if I were to throw it out?

- If I don't need this now, will I need it in the near future?

- If so, where might I stow it so that it is out of the way *and* accessible?

- Does this item imply a responsibility that no longer interests me? If so, does it get thrown out? And/or, to whom could I pass on both the item and its associated responsibility?

How your physical space looks determines how you use your mind. The cleaner your office, the cleaner your work will be. Plus, the clutter in your home impacts your state of mind when you come to work. Housecleaning matters. Really! I'm not saying there is a way, a particular standard, that is "right." I'm saying that there is a particular state of things that is right for you.

Area Two: Your Life Domains

Remember, all your Life Domains impact each other. Check your Life Domains (figure 4, page 84) at this time and note if there is anything that needs your attention in the next twelve to eighteen months. To reach your current goals, is there anything you need to address or clean up in the area of your

- Health or physical and mental well-being?

- Family and/or community?

- Personal development?

- Spirituality?

- Finances?

- Avocation?

Area Three: Your Short- and Long-Term Goals

Refer back to your "Goals" panel from chapter 2 and, in the spirit of having things clean and clear, take out a new sheet of paper. Set up a new "Goals" panel as you did the first. Keep the original for the time being; you will refer back to it. Now do the following:

- Reconsider your short-term goals and start a new list.

- Rewrite and refine the list, keeping only those that are still appropriate.

- Add any new twelve- to eighteen-month goals you have as a result of this or previous chapters.

I hope that now we've succeeded in broadening your view of the importance of removing the clutter around you, as well as looking at the time that's available from a new perspective. We've talked about what's important in each of the four life quarters. Through the exercise just completed, you may have begun to see for yourself the impact housecleaning can have on your ability to have the kinds of results you want in your life.

The next chapter is itself a revealing and useful multistage exercise, one that is at the very heart of the PaperRoom process. By the end of the chapter, you will have distinguished the things you will need to feel fulfilled at work and in life as well.

CHAPTER SIX

The Heart of Your Paper Room

Here's one of the biggest takeaways for me from the PaperRoom: I discovered that the main ingredient I needed in a job was to feel jazzed. The way I went about dissecting the ten best things in my life was just a great way to take pieces of life and extract the key learnings from them. What I learned was that I really need to work with a variety and a flow of people. I had been doing some investment work on my own, and was really unhappy. I found out the reason was that I wasn't interacting with people. Once I realized I needed people, I made sure I had one meeting every day with somebody, and that has made all the difference. — Julio

In this second of two
Focus chapters you will:

• *Discover and use the most powerful tool of the PaperRoom process, your TopTen*

• *Discover your needs and values and learn how to interpret and use them for your career*

• *Define the qualities of experience you need to be regenerated, fulfilled, and successful*

The TopTen: Creating the Career You Want

Why is it that on some days we feel absolutely invincible and capable of tackling anything, and on other days we can't imagine what on earth ever gave us that thought? How come one morning we think it's amusing that the woman in the next cubicle needs to call her kids every five minutes, but that very afternoon, we quietly contemplate how we can permanently hide her cell phone without being discovered? Why do we work so hard at masking our lack of confidence and tolerating the things that bother us, rather than looking for a solution?

I realize you may consider me far too optimistic, but through my work with clients in the PaperRoom, I have discovered that there *is* something we can do about all of this.

There is something we can do to be appropriately confident and less susceptible to the "mood of the moment." We've seen how our unrecognized habits and beliefs have limited our choices, and how our environment limits our actions. It is now time to discover how to use the same Results System and our Silent Partners to our advantage.

From time to time many of us feel uncomfortable with our work situation, but we haven't a clue what to do about it. Sometimes our discomfort is an indicator that we need to adjust something. It's time to learn something new, time to expand our professional toolbox and learn to work effectively with different people in different situations, time for a raise, time to take on a new project, or time to get organized and remember we have a life outside work. Other times our questioning heralds the need for new freedoms, life changes, and very different challenges. But how do we distinguish the need for a discreet change from the need for a fundamental change? How do we know exactly what is missing so we can fix it or replace it?

Common wisdom says that to discover the sort of work we should be doing, we need to look at our professional skills, strengths, and aptitudes and find a match. That is not wrong as far as it goes. But what do you do when you aren't ready financially or emotionally to stop working, yet the thought of facing the next twenty-plus years doing the same thing you have been doing for the last ten to thirty years is more than you can bear? What if you have no work history per se because you just got out of school or are just returning to the workforce, or if you simply want to do something completely different? And while we are looking at this, how come having a job that *does* utilize our skills, strengths, and aptitudes doesn't always fit the bill?

"You only live once, but if you work it right, once is enough."
—Joe E. Lewis, comedian

"My interest is in the future, because I'm going to be spending the rest of my life there."
—Charles Kettering, inventor

. **Getting Started**

The following exercise is designed to give you the ability to recognize and recover what is missing when you feel your confidence slipping and to identify a work environment that fits you, rather than you adapting to fit it. You will learn how to guard against burnout and find challenges that energize rather than exhaust your creativity. In this exercise you will discover what conditions need to be present for you to flourish professionally, regardless of what you choose to do, and how you can put those conditions in place. Sound too good to be true? Let's give it a try. Here's a hint of what you have in store for you, in Sylvia's words:

> *It's taken three years, and I'm doing it. I'm doing consulting and market research, researching ancient wisdom, and playing the flute. Consulting is my practice, "entrepreneuring" is my passion, research is my wisdom, and my soul is playing the flute, my vibrancy. That's what gets me excited and holds all the rest together. When I was nine I wanted to play the flute. And now I'm using it to balance my life!*

The TopTen Exercise

Completing this exercise will probably take a few hours. It is fine to do it a little at a time, always coming back to where you left off. I suggest that you read the instructions for each part only as you do that part. Reading through all the questions first is likely to diminish the value of the exercise for you.

Step 1 • Listing Your TopTen

Take an 8.5" x 11" piece of paper, turn it sideways, and fold it into four equal columns. Label the first column on the left "My TopTen."

MY TOPTEN	WHY?	CORE NEEDS	NEW ACTIONS

My TOPTEN
Family trip to Providence
White-water trip
Walking through the fields at my grandmother's house
Having my children
Falling in love
The road trip with Mark

(See the example on page 97 or download the "TopTen" panel at *www.thepaperroom.com*.)

In this first column, list ten really fabulous times or moments of your life. You don't need to rack your brain for the ten *best* times in your life. However, these should be times that were great enough so that if this were the last day of your life and you could relive any ten unique moments or times, these would be ten that you might choose. They can be written in any order (they need not be sequential in time or relative importance), and they can represent any length of time (a moment in time or a period of your life). They can be surprises, accomplishments, awards, discoveries, momentous first times, or any deeply meaningful positive events or moments such as "my senior high school prom," "riding horseback with Fred," "getting my driver's license," and so on.

The experiences should be different from each other. For instance, if you love travel and have taken many trips, pick the best of the best that shows why you love traveling. If you love parties, walks in the woods, tennis matches, or going to the symphony, put down a true example of the best, or best representative, of each kind of experience. Don't be concerned about getting exactly the right ones. Trust what your mind comes up with. It can be as simple as "Dad giving me popcorn at the movies."

By the way, some people think they can't possibly narrow their choices to only ten; the majority, however, think it's impossible to come up with that many. Trust me; you can do it.

Please finish step 1 before moving on to step 2.

Step 2 • Why?

Label your second column "Why?" For each of your ten experiences, ask yourself, "What was it about that experience that made it so important to me?" Why was it so special? Think about what it meant for you. Write some words and phrases that explain what made this event or time so valuable. For instance, if you wrote "Getting an 'A' in math" in your "TopTen" column, your

WHY?
Exploring and discovering things together.
Beautiful, spectacular setting; excitement; community
Safety; my spot; freedom
Huge shift to feeling confident/competent; sense of accomplishment, partnership
New beginning, feeling it will be there forever
Camaraderie, closeness; "real talk," really got to know him

"Why?" might be "I didn't think it was possible" or "He was the toughest teacher in the school," or "I showed them" or "I didn't know I was that good" (or all four of these comments). Or let's say you put "Hiking with my family on my tenth birthday" in your "TopTen" column. In the second column you might put "Connection with my Dad" or "My own physical strength" or "Reaching the summit after a long struggle."

If it looks like you're using the same words over and over, like "It was fun," go deeper. Why was it fun? Get specific about what really made that experience rewarding for you. What was your real prize? Let's say you put down "Giving the keynote address at the annual conference" and the first word that came to your mind describing that experience was "exhilarating." I would ask you, "Why, specifically, was it exhilarating?" And you might say, "It was exhilarating because it was the first time I ever got a standing ovation." It is fine to put a number of answers in your "Why?" column. Just keep questioning yourself on each TopTen event until you know you have gotten down to the root importance of each experience.

Please finish this section before reading on.

About Experiential Connectors

Let's take a minute now to talk about some things that will help you make the most of your TopTen exercise. Each of the things you mentioned in your "TopTen" column was an experience, a particularly memorable positive experience. If you will remember, when we first looked at the Results System in chapter 1, you learned that each experience registers cause-and-effect data to your Silent Partners. The results in the ten experiences you wrote down were positive. In previous chapters we talked mostly about the role our Silent Partners play by inhibiting our taking new actions or doing new things, and we've been learning how to avoid automatically doing things that currently may not be in our own best interest or that are negative in some way. Now you are learning about the conditions that automatically register positive information for you, and will learn how to use the tenacity of your Silent Partners to your best advantage.

The Meanings Behind the "Why?"

When you answered the question "Why?" in step 2, you were describing the effect or results of that kind of experience. Predictably, when something happens again that is like one of those TopTen experiences, your Results System will kick in and you will feel good about yourself and confident in the same way you did the first time it happened. We value these kinds of experiences because of the effect they have on us, and we need to be in environments where those same kinds of experiences can happen again. The reason we feel vulnerable—sometimes but not always—is in part because these feelings don't last forever. Whenever we experience burnout, or our natural ability to navigate life with style and grace is weakened, what we need is to repeat one of our TopTen affirming experiences. But repeating the exact experience of, for example, Fred asking you to the prom or climbing Kilimanjaro is not likely to happen on a regular basis. What can you do about this?

Magic in the Metaphors

Your TopTen affirming experiences are actually metaphors for particular kinds of positive experiences. When you wrote down *why* that event was important to you, you began to identify the reasons the experience was valuable to you. In the future, you only need to have an experience that your Silent Partners see as similar to your TopTen event to experience the same positive feelings about yourself as you did in the original event. Tony said it well:

> *One of my TopTens was going fishing with Dad. It was quiet, we were alone, we laughed a lot. As I thought about that experience and tried to figure out which TopTen "Why?" category it belonged in, I saw that for me it was about connection and recognition. Then when I was trying to think about what other things in my life gave me the same feeling, I thought about having lunch with John—he's my boss.*

Step 3 • Revealing Your Core Needs

Move to the third column on the panel and label it "Core Needs." All our core needs are intimately connected to our values; each one points to some quality and/or experience we value highly. Our core needs fall into four distinct categories: *challenge, recognition, accomplishment,* and *connection.* These categories often can be further defined or refined by grouping them into who or what they involve: *others, things, ideas,* or *self.*

In the "Core Needs" column you're going a bit deeper to expand your understanding of the reasons you found your TopTen important. Here you will gain a deeper insight into the essence of your needs and values. Before you begin to work on this section it is important to understand what you are going to be doing and why.

In this column you will distill your information further so that you will finally put names to your personal needs and values. The things you need are the things you value. The good news is that your Silent Partners need only the same sort of experience—not the same event—to give you the positive experience you are looking for.

If this is beginning to look daunting, don't worry. It will not be as difficult or complicated as it might seem. You may think you will need help from someone to get the right answers, but you won't. Only you know the essence of each experience, even if you don't yet have the right words for it. We are going to take this one step at a time. Have fun with it. Do it in a number of sittings, if that's what works best for you. This isn't a race; it's an exploration, and each time you come back to it you will see even more. The results will be worth it. After all, this is your career and your life.

The following definitions and examples may help you begin to identify your core needs and values. Use any of the synonyms, related words, or their variations to describe needs and values in column three, or you may come up with a few of your own.

Chal·lenge

Definition

- *(v)* To confront or defy boldly

- *(v)* To arouse or stimulate especially by presenting with difficulties

- *(v)* To make or present a challenge

- *(n)* A stimulating task or problem (*looking for new* challenges)

Synonym

(v) To dare: to call out to duel or combat, to invite into competition

Related words

brave, defy, double-dog dare, front, out-dare, venture, arouse, awaken, bestir, kindle, rally, rouse, wake, waken, whet

Your First Core Need: Challenge

Challenging Environments   Some people have a need to be in actual challenging environments in order to be challenged, while others do not (example: a dot-com startup versus a research project). Challenges can come from people, situations, ideas, or things. The people who need challenging environments often have comments in the "Why?" column such as:

- "Nobody thought I could do it"

- "They thought it was impossible"

- "I wanted to see if I could"

- "I was the first" (best, smartest, quickest, etc.)

Testing Your Mettle   The previous examples are all challenges to beat the odds. If these statements sound like ones you would make, you are someone who needs to take on one or two things that are "impossible" from time to time. Eighty percent of the satisfaction you get from those endeavors is testing your mettle and going for it. The satisfaction you are seeking is not so much the result—winning the road race—although that is clearly the goal. Your satisfaction comes from the mastery with which you drove the car and the moment-to-moment finesse of your moves. The nugget of gold we find in being successfully challenged is the release of our creativity. The satisfaction that comes from stretching outside our comfort zone, learning something new about ourselves, and touching some new level of mastery is always rewarding.

Just Any Old Challenge Will Not Do   The right type of challenge is one that releases your ability to stretch, not one that stops you dead in the water. For instance, a person might feel exhilarated by the challenge of coordinating a series of interoffice productivity workshops, yet feel sorely (as in *painfully*) challenged by delivering a speech at the annual conference. Can you feel the difference? Can you think of challenges that excite you as opposed to those that make you squirm? There is no need to make this business of succeeding and living life fully more painful or difficult, even though some of us seem to have inherited a legacy of valuing struggle.

Supportive Environments People who need to be challenged in environments that are not in and of themselves challenging generally flourish in an environment of support with encouraging comments like these:

- "You can do it!"

- "If anyone can do it, you can!"

- "Hey, I think you are crazy, but go for it!"

When you answer the question of whether each event was challenging, you are looking for the condition that compelled you to take action. Do you do your best work when you are offered a reward? Or is it something thought to be impossible that gets you going?

Challenge Activity Reread the description of the word *challenge* and note in your third column each of your TopTen events that was a challenge.

Rec·og·ni·tion

Definition

• The action of recognizing: the state of being recognized

• The knowledge or feeling that someone or something present has been encountered before; special notice or attention

Synonym

Discovery: the act or process of achieving self-knowledge; a learning process that relates a perception of something new to knowledge already possessed

Related words

cognizance, realization, awareness, consciousness, sensibility

Your Second Core Need: Recognition

Birth Order I have seen in the PaperRoom that birth order often has a lot to do with the kinds of recognition we need. Take a few moments to notice how you were "recognized" in your family of origin.

First and only children often need to be recognized as "first" or "foremost." They are often leaders or take roles that have them stand out from the crowd. Statistics say that families predictably see second children as "risk takers," and I have seen that even if they seem extraordinarily conventional, they may have chosen to live life differently from their parents, and so are seen by their family as taking risks. Middle children, I've noticed, often like the recognition gained by doing things that boldly draw attention to themselves. For many, it seems that the need for assurance that they are "really there" is deeply felt throughout their lives. Last, or later, children are often less concerned about having to please or be recognized in some particular way by others and are more likely to want experiences in which they recognize themselves and to be in touch with a certain kind of independence. Do you think your birth order has something to do with how you like or need to be recognized?

Self-Recognition It is important for all of us to feel known or recognized. I'm not referring to being famous, but to an affirmation of self, a reflection of who we experience ourself to be. This can have the quality of suddenly recognizing your unique talent, a personality trait, or strength. It can feel like meeting yourself face to face. And it can happen either through others recognizing you or through an experience of self-recognition. It is important for each of us to discover what conditions we need to best recognize our own mastery.

Recognition Activity Reread the description of the word *recognition*. In your third column, for each of your TopTen events that were "recognitions" note anything that you think had to do with recognition of the real you, either by others or by yourself, or perhaps both.

Ac·com·plish·ment

Definition

• Something completed or effected

• An acquired excellence or skill

Synonym

Achievement: a quality or ability equipping one for society; a special skill or ability acquired by training or practice

Related words

action, act, deed, attainment, completion, acquirement, acquisition, finish

Your Third Core Need: Accomplishment

A Positive Sense of Self You would think that if there were one thing we would be aware of, it would be our accomplishments. Yet what we all seem to forget, and in some cases never see, are the majority of our accomplishments. For someone who has lived fifty years or so, the compiled list would be daunting; even for twenty years it can be formidable. You are the sum total of all your accomplishments, but they certainly will not all show up on your TopTen list. The accomplishments that are likely to appear in your Top-Ten are those that have most validated your positive sense of self.

Closure The experience of accomplishment is closure. This has to do with the satisfaction of finishing something, as distinct from the pleasure of recognition. Things like applause, awards, and great report cards and reviews have a more important role than simply being complimentary. They are public affirmations that you finished what you said you would do. They let you know the job is done. If you have such experiences in your TopTen, it will be important for you to have one or two projects going that have a clear beginning, middle, and end.

A great example is Nina. She is a nurse who had "Getting a standing ovation" for her performance in a play in high school as one of her TopTen events. At the time she did the PaperRoom, she talked to me about how uncomfortable she felt telling me about it. She said it felt too much like bragging, and that she didn't really like being the center of attention. Two years later when I interviewed her for this book, here's what she said:

> *When the good stuff happens now, I recognize it's one of my TopTen. I say, "Aha, there it is," and there's comfort in that. I know that the particular moment is really right for me. For instance, before I would have been embarrassed when I got the big compliments, but now I can take it in. Now I'm conscious of who I really am and I let myself enjoy it.*

Often things that were valued as challenges become accomplishments, but their relative importance for your needs and values is how you spoke about them when you first remembered them and wrote them down on your TopTen list. Challenges speak to a certain kind of beginning, whereas accomplishments speak to the result. What sorts of accomplishments do you have on your list? Is who knows about them, or who comments on them, important? If so, what do these people represent? Are they respected "older people," peers, individuals, or groups? Or yourself?

Accomplishment Activity Take some time now and glean all the accomplishments you can find from your TopTen. Include the items you may have already marked as "recognition" items that you now recognize as accomplishments. Remember that each TopTen event may satisfy several needs.

Con·nec·tion

Definition

• A relation of personal intimacy (as of family ties)

• A person connected with another, especially by marriage, kinship, or common interest

• A political, social, professional, or commercial relationship

Synonyms

Relation, link, bond, association

Community

A unified body of individuals; a group of people with common characteristics or interests living together within a larger society or in a particular area; an interacting population of various kinds of individuals in a common location

Related words

affiliation, alliance, combination, conjoinment, conjunction, hookup, partnership, tie-up, togetherness

Your Fourth Core Need: Connection

Others and Self We generally recognize the need to be connected to family, friends, and community. Connection is usually thought of as being connected to others, but we also have a need to be connected to ourself. Most of us spend a good deal of our life stretching our limits in one way or another. We stretch our time, we stretch our ability to handle situations, and we stretch to understand others. Like a rubber band, if we stay extended for too long, we will fray and break. We need to retract and refuel, to quietly get "regrounded." These moments of connecting with ourself renew and replenish us so that we can stretch again.

Environment People are often influenced positively or negatively by their physical environment. If you love having beauty around you, you aren't necessarily an avid consumer or a person who is interested only in superficial things. It may be that it gives you a sense of well-being to see things that please your eye. It's actually important to have your work space be pleasing to you. The subtle and not-so-subtle messages we pick up with all our senses play a major role in how we feel about our day.

Quiet Moments An important aspect of connection to self is the need to tune out the static of daily life, to take a breath, take a break. The kinds of things you might have in your TopTen that point to this need are quiet moments, often in nature. When we take even a momentary respite from daily activities, we regain our sense of self. Do you have an event on your TopTen list that reconnects you to your sense of self? Notice which experiences in your TopTen have connected you to others and which have connected you to yourself.

Any event can be a vastly different experience for different people. This includes getting a new job, leaving your parental home, writing poetry, anything. You are the only one who can say what each of your TopTen events fundamentally means to and for you. If an experience satisfied a number of needs, list only the most important.

Connection Activity Now go down your TopTen list and note which events satisfied a need for connection of some sort. The example on the facing page shows what the columns may begin to look like.

Some Other Clues to Identifying Your Needs and Values

As I have said, any particular experience or event can satisfy more than one need. Here is an example: giving birth to children. You may find that for you, giving birth was important because it was a new project, a new arena for learning and growing. In this case "challenge" may be a fit for you. Or, if you loved the actual birth experience, it may have been a time when you connected with yourself, when you experienced the act of creation in a personal, private way. If so, you would have had an experience of "connection" with yourself. Likewise, if an aspect of the experience was that you loved sharing and creating this experience together with your spouse, that would be a connection of another sort. And it may well have been a time when you felt the profound accomplishment of producing another living being. By the way, women are not the only people who speak about the birth of their children as a TopTen event—men do, too. And here is another interesting fact: the overwhelming majority of people who do have something about the birth of children on their TopTen list are entrepreneurs. See any connection there?

Other commonly mentioned TopTen events with many layers of richness are annual family gatherings—religious and other holidays, summers on the beach, family trips, and so on. When we look into our professional lives for the reflection of these kinds of events, they can show up as annual company picnics, seasonal events like the crunch at tax time if you are an accountant, inventory or sale time if you are in the retail business. Some of the core feelings that family events represent involve the experience of belonging, camaraderie, and a sense of shared history. If you have two or three events involving others in this way, you will either want to work in a relatively established organization or belong to work-related associations—something that can predictably give you the experience of a "family gathering" from time to time in the ways you most enjoy experiencing it. The occasional impromptu after-work get-together might do the trick.

MY TOPTEN	WHY?	CORE NEEDS	NEW ACTIONS
1 Family trip to Providence	Exploring and discovering things together	Connection: accomplishment and discovery	Going to that new restaurant with Ellen & Joan
2 White-water trip	Beautiful, spectacular community	Accomplishment, challenge, connection	Taking that metal sculpture art class
3 Walking through the fields at my grandmother's house	Safety, my spot, freedom	Connection, individualization	Closing my office door, opening the window, not doing a darned thing!
4 Having my children	Huge change to something I felt confident/competent about; sense of accomplishment; partnership	Beginnings; connection; recognition	Agreeing to run the Book Fair this year
5 Falling in love	New beginning—feeling it would be there forever	Beginnings; recognition; connection; accomplishment	Moving to Santa Fe!
6 The road trip with Mark	Camaraderie; closeness; "real talk," really got to know him, changed our relationship forever	Connection, discovery; recognition	Give Richard a call... go see a movie, go to the museum

Travel and vacations of many different kinds are often on TopTen lists, and they often fulfill a multitude of needs and values; some of these can certainly be duplicated at work. If you have travel or a vacation on your list, notice if it involves going to something—learning something new, discovering, doing different things, and so on—or getting *away from* something. The need to get away can sometimes be satisfied by closing your office door if you have one, or taking an afternoon off. But sometimes wanting a vacation is just that—a need to get away.

Step 4: • New Actions

When you have completed your third column, you can label the fourth column "New Actions." We'll fill it in later. The next chapters will give you new information that will help you do a better job with this last column. You won't be transforming all these insights into action until you've completed chapter 9, which will help you move forward and keep you on track with your goals. But first there is a little more cleaning up to do, followed by switching your life-lens to a wider angle.

Maintaining Your Sense of Self

Armed with new insights into your needs and values, you have some new tools to help you maintain the confidence, or sense of self, you need to think through and ride out the bumps in life. As you become familiar with how this skill can work for you and become facile in implementing it, you will be better able to cope with problems and establish an environment that supports you. Next we will begin to fine-tune your navigation skills and gain some valuable insights by looking at your work history. You will learn to identify what you need in a work environment and begin to see how to go about getting it.

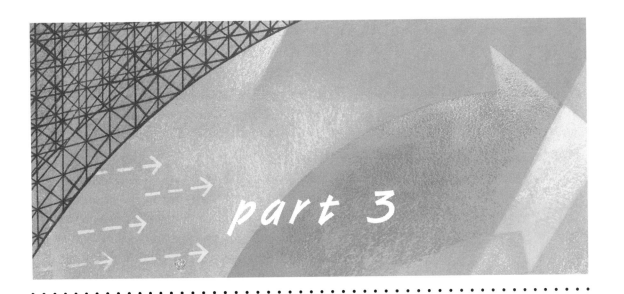

part 3

ACT

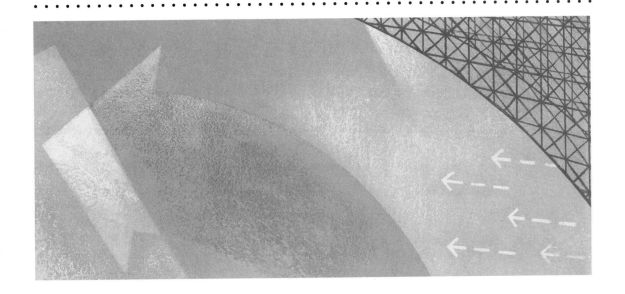

CHAPTER SEVEN

Navigation Skills

Some time after the PaperRoom, I got an opportunity to be hired as an employee for the company I'd been consulting with. Even though it meant giving up my success and freedom as a consultant, I took the job; I used what I'd learned from the PaperRoom, and I realized this job had all the elements of what I'd learned I needed. It turned out to be really wonderful. The elements of the position were my needs and values, what I now could see I needed to feed me—pioneering, learning, adventure, and freedom to explore. — Cam

*In this first of four
Action chapters you will:*

- *Determine the elements you need to thrive in your work environment*

- *Discover how you know when your core needs aren't being fulfilled*

- *Practice identifying your needs and creating the experience you want*

Controlling Your Destiny

N othing is quite as sweet as the rewards enjoyed after considerable effort. Having gotten this far in the book, you should know quite a bit more about yourself and how "your system" operates. At this point you should be seeing some new possibilities or openings where you hadn't realized they existed. In the remaining chapters we will gather the information you have worked on thus far and learn how to apply it. These chapters have the tools you need to navigate your professional life with greater certainty—less at the mercy of circumstances and more in control of your destiny and the quality of your life. See what Kim has achieved using her PaperRoom tools:

Since the PaperRoom, my career life has changed quite a bit. Overall, I have a lot more confidence and am making the choices that are good for me, even though they're not conventional. Socially, or in my family, they might be questioned, but they feel right to me. I have no doubts about the decisions I'm making. I am managing my own career. Before, even though I am smart and well educated, I could never find a job where I was comfortable and happy. Now I'm making more money than before and I'm happy in my work. I had left a job working for a large investment company because the environment didn't fit. Then, during the process of the PaperRoom, I realized that a job that would really work for me would be as a tour guide. I had learned from the PaperRoom process that, whatever I was doing, I needed to be totally in charge from beginning to end, and I needed to be in an active environment, so now I have my own tour business. This summer was my second season doing that and it feels so good! It fits so well with who I am. Unbelievable. My gosh, I feel like an old pro. During the winter I have my own private practice as an investment consultant. I'm happy, and my businesses are thriving, too!

In this chapter we are going to use information from three previous chapters. We'll work with and complete your "TopTen" panel from chapter 6, using the "Me" section from chapter 3 about how you saw yourself in your family, and reviewing some information from your work on your "Patterns" panel from chapter 4. By the end of this chapter you will have some new tools to help you recognize when one of your core needs is not being fulfilled and correct the problem. Let's get started.

Using "Me" (from Chapter 3)

The ways we thought about ourselves as kids—who we thought we were, what we thought we were like—was primarily influenced by our parental figures. They were the most important people in our life and our first connection to the world. It was not until we were teenagers and began to question their authority and differentiate and prioritize things in the world that we began to acquire some new "truths" of our own. It's interesting to note that how you thought about yourself then or how others thought of you then still often forms the basis of how you think about yourself now. For instance, if, when you were a child, your important two or three adults thought you were smart, funny, well-behaved, and responsible, and you felt smart, funny, well-behaved, and responsible with them, today you wouldn't bat an eye if you met someone who thought you weren't too bright, had no sense of humor, and were obnoxious and irresponsible. You would realize that the person just really doesn't know you. Take a look at your list and see if that isn't true for you.

The things that only one person thought about you will be things that are sometimes but not always true for you. For instance, John felt he was an interesting person around his mother, but he believed there was nothing interesting he could say when he was with his dad. Today John thinks, "Sometimes I'm interesting to others, and sometimes I'm not."

Identifying Work Environments

Identifying the characteristics others saw in you as you were growing up and noticing your reaction to others' perceptions will give you two important methods for tackling the next task. However you determined the characteristics that felt right to you, awareness of them now will give you a guide to identifying and recognizing work environments in which you will be comfortable and valued (or not).

Finding the right place to work when you know how you see yourself is comparatively easy; work in an environment that needs a person just like you for the job. We spend far too much time trying to be someone we are not, just because we happen to have the skills the organization is looking for. We generally focus on what we can do, what we are experienced in, and who will hire us. We forget to consider seriously whether the environment is complementary to our preferred working style and personality. Jen does not forget:

> *I think about this PaperRoom stuff a lot—I use it as a yardstick. I'm about to begin another job search, and as I decide how to move forward, my needs and values are at the forefront of my thinking so that I can be sure that I'll be happy. In defining this new job, I'll be making sure that it aligns with my needs and values. I'm making sure it is a job where I can overdeliver and get big results. The way I'm doing this job search is a direct result of the work in the PaperRoom.*

If, for example, people thought you were funny and that felt right to you, you need to work in an environment in which people like your kind of humor and think you are a great addition to the team because of it. If people thought you were bossy, and you agree, get yourself a job where "bossy" is a good thing and people are thrilled with your ability to "tell it like it is" and not "beat around the bush." Laura's story is a perfect example.

Laura did the PaperRoom a few years ago. It was clear that she was great at meeting targets, managing the stock, and making sure things ran smoothly, but she didn't have good people skills. She was considered too bossy. Though she loved the ready-to-wear business, her bossiness had kept her professionally stuck at the level of assistant department manager. When we fast-forward to the results of her discoveries in the PaperRoom, Laura left retailing and took her reliability, ability to deliver on time and on target, and considerable visual skills into a new profession. She became a building renovation contractor. She was no longer perceived as bossy; she was highly valued and respected for "having the guts" to hold the line and do what was needed to get the job done. "And," her colleagues said, "she's even a *woman!*" She loved it!

Reviewing Past Work Environments

In which jobs did you feel most comfortable or appreciated?

Go back to your "Patterns" panel from chapter 3 now and review the jobs you enjoyed. Did they enjoy you? Comfortably fitting in and/or being appreciated for who you are is very different from having or not having the skills necessary to do the job. Both employers and employees may overlook this difference, and it is often at the core of what is really missing in the job for both of them.

Avoiding Burnout The second reason we looked at how you felt as a kid is a bit more complicated but is absolutely key to your staying the course, not burning out, and having the ability to meet challenges head-on. This is how it works. First we need to get back to the Results System we introduced in chapter 1, the invisible perceptions, beliefs, habits, expectations, and assumptions that lie just below the surface of your consciousness and are always ready to leap into action. We discussed how our Silent Partners are there to ensure our "survival." If we lived through an event by doing something or by reacting in a particular way, our Results System sees this as being successful. When we repeat this behavior a few times with the same results, our actions become invisible to us. From then on we continue that behavior without having to think about it. This happens whether or not we liked the event. The system lets us remember how to get through things—but it is not concerned with the quality of our experience. Are you beginning to see the wisdom of the old adage "Learn it right the first time"?

When Core Needs Aren't Fulfilled So how does this invisible behavior work with our core needs that we identified in chapter 6? As we grow and become more experienced, we learn a variety of solutions for fulfilling our core needs. We build up a collection of solutions, or acceptable actions or reactions to a particular circumstance. If we don't succeed from the very beginning at fulfilling a need, we continue to search through our storehouse of previous solutions for one that will work in this situation. If this goes on long enough, eventually we arrive at that "survival behavior" we exhibited as a kid. This first learned behavior or reaction is our "default behavior." It is also a clue that we have a core need that has gone unfulfilled for too long. Another way to say this is that when we don't get what we want or need, we act like a child!

As long as our needs and values are fulfilled, we feel great and can take on challenges and be relatively patient adults when things don't go as we wish. When one or more of our needs and/or values have gone past their expiration date, we begin to doubt ourselves, and old coping behaviors return. In these moments we are reverting to unconscious ways of reacting as we did in the past. The Results System itself is just an automatic device; it doesn't know what response will serve you now. The longer we wait for the right validating experience to show up, the further we retreat into those old behaviors.

For example, I love challenges but I'm not very keen on incentives. If you try to challenge me by telling me I will get some sort of reward if I do this or that, I actually find it difficult to do the work. Sales incentives make the task unpleasant, and the longer I work at them, the worse I seem to get and the

> *"Leftover traumas can be incentives for innovation and change [so we can] free the lover and jester inside us all."*
> —**Louise J. Kaplan, therapist and author**

unhappier I am with the job. I procrastinate; I come up with excuses; I pray for rain—*anything* not to do the job! If, on the other hand, you tell me something is "impossible," wild horses couldn't hold me back. Before I discovered this, I could never understand why I was so good at getting things to happen and so bad at sales. Normally when faced with a task, we think our only choice is to try harder, wait it out, and do our best not to show our displeasure or annoyance. Now, with some practice, you will be able to identify the real problem and control the situation more effectively.

In Charge of Your System

You now have the tools to identify exactly what is missing. Your core needs from the "TopTen" exercise give you access to the heart of your Results System and the ability to manage it, rather than having your system manage you. Following is how it works in a little more detail.

When one of our core needs, such as the need to be recognized in a particular way, goes unfulfilled for too long, we begin to act out in ways similar to those that have gotten us the desired recognition in the past. Leslie is a good example.

The Manager

Leslie managed an administrative department in a local hospital. She had been there for years and was considered competent, but she had a "bad attitude." This had apparently escalated to the point where she was in danger of losing her job. To make a very long story short, when Leslie did the PaperRoom we saw that her "bad attitude" was the way she had acted as a kid when she thought her older sister was getting something she wasn't. Leslie thought her sister was the favorite and got all the attention, so most of what her sister got made Leslie mad. Interestingly, at work Leslie felt unappreciated. It seemed to her that "everyone else got the credit for doing things."

To solve the problem, Leslie and her boss set up a regular time each month to go over what had been accomplished and the plans for the coming month. I have no idea whether Leslie's boss was actually giving anyone else more attention than Leslie, but the monthly meetings satisfied Leslie's need to be singled out and got her boss to focus on her work in a positive way. Her "bad attitude" disappeared.

With the help of the same tools you are now learning to use, Leslie recognized she was acting as she had as a kid, then identified on her list of core needs exactly what was missing that had triggered that childhood reaction. It was only then that she was able to take an appropriate action at work to provide what had been missing.

If you recall, the purpose of knowing your core needs is to understand the kinds of feedback you need occasionally to maintain your confidence so you can then step forward into life rather than retreat. Let's look at a time when you were in retreat, identify what need was not being met, and then see what could replace it to get you back on a roll again.

Your Unanswered Needs

Think of a specific time in the fairly recent past when you were upset about something or not feeling at the top of your game.

1. **Identify the behavior.** Remember how you felt, how you were acting. Identify what childhood behavior had been triggered. Generally it will show up as an exaggeration of one of the traits attributed to you in the "Family" panel (p. 58).

2. **Identify the need.** Now go over to your TopTen and "try on" each of your TopTen experiences. You are looking for events on your TopTen list that make you think, "I haven't felt like *that* in a long time." Only one, or perhaps two, will give you a bit of a tug and seem like a particularly welcome idea. Highlight or flag it on your TopTen list.

3. **"Recreate" the experience.** Take out your TopTen panel from Chapter 6, page 97. It is time to complete your "New Actions" column. Think of one or two actions you could take that would bring whatever is missing back into your life. It doesn't have to be big. Leslie simply had to arrange meetings with her boss. She didn't have to solve her childhood problem. Whatever action(s) you choose, it simply has to give you the experience you currently need.

You can use this process whenever you feel "something is not right" or when you find yourself acting out in a way that isn't working.

You've just determined what you need in a job; you've learned the signs of unfulfilled core needs; and you've practiced using your needs to create a fulfilling work experience for yourself. Next you will sharpen your skills at working with your Silent Partners by using your new knowledge and tools on a real test project in your life.

CHAPTER EIGHT

Working the System

. . . .

I'm managing my time better, making sure that what I do adds to my quality of life. So I let go of whatever is in my life that's not contributing to that. I'm more aware of what I do with my life and the choices I make [as] I navigate through life. I see what is good for me, what is healthy, and how to meet the needs that I have. Then I balance the time that I have for work, play, and community. I like work. I have to make conscious decisions about what direction I'm going—it's up to me to know when it's time for something different. I know what I need and want and I own that. No one is going to take that from me. — Ina

. . . .

In this second of four
Action chapters you will:

- *Practice your new skills to detect and circumvent your Silent Partners*

- *Try your new skills on a real test project in your life. This chapter can be your training wheels. You'll become familiar with your Silent Partners in a much more intimate way.*

Applying Your New Skills

Changing the way we are used to doing things is harder work than we think it should be. There's no way around it. The speed and ease of the task fall far short of our hopes and expectations. What it takes is having a way to:

- Remember what was previously an unconscious act (driven by our Silent Partners)

- Remember to do it in the new way

- Repeatedly do it in the new way long enough to see the rewards and to have the new behavior become as comfortable—as invisible—as the original behavior

Fortunately, there is a way.

Hearing Your Silent Partners

In this chapter you will sharpen your ability to recognize when your Silent Partners have taken over. You may be amazed by how clever and tenacious they are in their effort to keep things the same. In chapter 1 we discussed the Silent Partners' three lines of defense: (1) being invisible; (2) giving you some good reasons why a possible action won't work, why you shouldn't do it, or at least why you shouldn't do it now; and (3) making the new or changed action feel uncomfortable. Since many of these beliefs were formed during childhood, you may want to review the information you gathered in chapter 3 when you recorded how you saw the perceptions, beliefs, habits, expectations, and assumptions about family and others, as well as any personal discoveries you may have made at that time.

But that's not all that's holding you back. Most of us live with self-defeating beliefs as though they were truths.

Common Self-Defeating Beliefs

Self-defeating beliefs are part of our culture and go hand in hand with our Silent Partners. They lead the way without us even noticing, and we meekly agree, saying, "Yes, that *is* true." Let's check them out.

1. "Success is progressing steadily up the career ladder."

    Conventional wisdom holds that a good résumé should reflect a career that has unfolded seamlessly on a predictable, logical uphill path. That's nonsense. It doesn't make sense that each truly valuable person has done only one thing all his or her professional life. Everyone's experience, regardless of how far-flung or seemingly unconnected, enriches each season of his or her career. Each experience forms the foundation for the next, even if it's in an entirely different direction. It's all learning. Nothing is an accident.

"Actions form habits; habits decide character; and character fixes our destiny."
—**Tyron Edwards, theologian**

"Existing society takes [it] for granted: that organizations outlive workers, and that people stay put. But today the opposite is true."
—**Peter Drucker, business futurist**

I know that each new venture and career experience I have had was homework for what I do now. Each job I have tackled, client I have had, and seminar I have delivered has deepened my understanding and broadened the scope of my ability to practice my craft. I see this phenomenon over and over again with my clients. How can a person grow, evolve, improve, and develop with any depth if he or she has been limited to only one narrow perspective stemming from one kind of experience? Innovation, creativity, and ultimately success in a career and a life are the products of thoughtful exploration and risk taking.

2.   "There's only one right way to . . . "

Well, maybe there used to be only one way, but not anymore. We are all pioneers, regardless of our chosen career or current life stage. Past generations did not have to deal with the realities and the choices open to us now. Even if you just got out of school, there are opportunities you could not have studied or prepared yourself for. Regardless of your time of life, you couldn't have anticipated today looking quite as it does. Few of us can find a role model to show us the way. Certainly there are some role models for some things, but often there really is no one precedent and no one right way. We can definitely be informed by the past, but it is unlikely that we could or would even want to repeat it. Better for us to do what seems best for now, to keep our eyes open and stay with a particular direction only as long as it makes sense to do so.

3.   "I need to know my decisions will work out before I make them."

If your decision is to do something you have never done before, it is of course important to do your homework, research, play out possible scenarios, know what you will do if it doesn't work out, and so forth. Regardless of the planning and the groundwork you lay, however, your new decision will never feel perfectly good or right at the right time, until after you do it.

"There are many ways of going forward, but only one way of standing still."
—**Franklin D. Roosevelt, U.S. president**

"Lead your; life don't follow it around."
—**Ken Kesey, author**

When you say you need to know first that the new decision will work out, what you're really saying is that you want to wait until you aren't afraid to do it. When you are trying something completely new to you, that will rarely be the case. You must pack "afraid" in your suitcase and take it along.

4. "The right choices are made objectively with a clear plan."

Objectivity and a clear plan are important ingredients to be sure, but today I can tell you that the most essential ingredient for making successful major career choices is rigorously honoring your own standards, your own deepest beliefs about what is right and what has integrity for you. When I was younger, I did not know the importance of acting on what is important at each stage of life. I can now see that the positive qualities of my life today are the result of the integrity of the decisions I made. You can do it—you always can—you just need to be willing to do it differently than you may have in the past, do it the best that you can, and understand that it probably isn't going to be perfect. Look before you leap . . . but definitely leap.

> "Life is about not knowing, making the best of [the moment] without knowing what's . . . next."
> —Gilda Radner, performer

5. "Success means getting the life you envisioned."

I have always believed that dreams really can come true. We do have control over our career—if not completely, at least far more than we recognize. However, it turns out it is a bit more complicated than I had first thought. We can get what we want, but it may not necessarily look the way we imagined it would look. "Success" doesn't always come in the package we expected. Remember, I had always pictured myself in that tile-roofed home in California. It took ten years for it to dawn on me that this antique colonial I live in now fits the bill perfectly. I used to think that having a successful career meant doing one thing and that I would have to choose. Now I see my work as a series of projects—some are "professional," some are "personal," all are challenging in different ways.

> "Life is what we make it. Always has been, always will be."
> —Grandma Moses, artist

All of them let me stretch different parts of myself. Spinning several dishes in the air at once is perfect for me. I love it!

6.   "There are many things I simply can't risk or attempt."

When we say we "can't" do something, 90 percent of the time it simply is not true. We may not know how, we may need support of some sort, we may need to learn something we don't currently know, or we may feel that the perceived cost is too great for the payoff. "I don't want to" or "I'm not sure I can" are better than "I can't" and probably closer to the truth. Here is why saying "can't" is a problem. When we tell ourselves something, generally we listen. When we say we can't do something, we effectively close off our options to explore any further. Don't sell yourself short. Be clear with yourself—tell yourself the truth. It will give you power and dignity and strength.

7.   "I'm not good with change."

Once and for all, let's resolve this issue about change. Stop being concerned—it is not a problem. We do it all the time; we just don't call it "change." How do you feel about wearing something new? How do you feel about going on a vacation, reading a new book, learning how to do the latest dance step? Is getting all that new stuff for your birthday a problem? Or that massage, which you would never have gotten for yourself? The skill we use when we embrace the things we want to do, have, or be are the same skills we engage when we need or want to change, but we call it "get to," as in, we "get to go on a vacation." We see it as an opportunity, a privilege, a long-anticipated occasion for celebration. If a problem does arise when you're faced with the option of change, you are probably paying too much attention to one of your Silent Partners. Silent Partners are real killjoys. As the saying goes, "Don't go there!" Instead, check in with yourself and what you've learned in the PaperRoom.

What is "right" for you?

_____

_____

_____

_____

"Change is the constant, the signal for rebirth, the egg of the phoenix."

—Christina Baldwin, healer and writer

Creating New Habits

Now go back to your short-term goals from chapter 2 and designate a project to use as a test case to learn to recognize the voice of your Silent Partners and learn to resist their influence. Look for a new habit you genuinely want to have, but one that is not at the top of your list in urgency. You don't need to take on the world at first; start with something relatively painless that looks manageable. If you don't think you have something on your list that fills that description, some other suggestions might be:

- Leaving work on time

- Remembering to eat lunch or breakfast

- Finishing a weekly report the day before it is due

- Exercising at least four times each week

The test project needs to be a new, ongoing physical habit you want to develop versus a one-time thing that you want to start, stop, or resolve. Pick something clearly defined that should or could happen at a specific time daily. It also should not be something that involves other people. You will want to make this as simple as possible. You are using a physical example because it is the easiest to work on and to see. Later you will be able to use what you learned to change many other kinds of habits such as thinking, hearing, and speaking.

In the PaperRoom, when people have difficulty coming up with something, I often suggest they empty their e-mail inbox every morning and at least acknowledge all the notes that others would want to know they received. Even if you can't address it at the moment, a quick "Got it" and "Will get back to you" does the trick. It's something that can be important to do regularly, if only for your peace of mind (and theirs), and many of us don't do it on a regular basis. It is also a good learning project because, in addition to being something we "should" do, it will be obvious when we forget to do it. The project you pick needs to be one where a change is obvious enough for you to easily recognize when you have established the new pattern. The final requirement is that this new habit be desirable enough to keep you interested, but not so important that not developing it will seriously affect you in any way. E-mail is a good choice because we are generally not so attached to the issue of e-mail clutter that we will have to deal with feelings of failure and low self-esteem if we occasionally forget during the learning process—which we will.

The Test Project Setup

The immediate goal, obviously, is to acquire a new habit. The invaluable purpose, however, is to learn how your Silent Partners work and how to recognize and disempower them. Following these suggested steps will help you with both your goal and your purpose.

1. **Pick a project** that fulfills the above criteria.

2. **Establish a regular time** for your project.

3. **Get materials** if needed.

4. **Adjust your calendar** or schedule to free up the time it will take.

5. **Inform people** who might need to know about your changes.

6. **Leave an *unavoidable* reminder** for yourself.

That last one is tricky. As you remember from chapter 1, invisibility is the Results System's first line of defense. Objects in your home or office environment "disappear" fairly quickly; for example, a reminder note on your computer screen might work for a few days, but then it will no longer attract your attention because it will look "normal" and won't catch your eye. Your reminder needs to be unavoidable and in your way enough so that you must deliberately try to avoid it. If your goal is to take time out for lunch daily, setting an alarm that you have to get up to turn off should do the trick.

Taking Action

Track the following two important items and keep notes. Keep whatever you are going to use to take notes on in a handy place. A 3" x 5" card in your pocket could work.

1. Listen for and jot down the excuses you use to try to postpone or eliminate your task. You may begin to notice that you use the same handful of reasons to avoid things. "I'll do it later," "I don't have time," and "This [whatever you are doing at the moment] is more important," are pretty common, but we each have our favorites. "I don't want to" works amazingly well for me; you'd think I was a petulant five-year-old!

2. Notice and jot down your feelings, such as impatience, anxiety, frustration, and so on, when you remember to do the new task. Feelings and the accompanying physical sensations you experience when you begin to try to change things from the way they have always been come from your Silent Partners. These feelings and sensations cause behavior that is aligned with the past rather than with your new resolve. Force yourself to do the task in spite of the discomfort.

As you practice, try to become increasingly familiar with your excuse phrases and the associated feelings you have when you do the new task anyway. You will probably notice that you use the same excuses—or the same kinds of excuses—all the time. The feelings associated with going against the dictates of your Silent Partners will be the same or similar as well. As you proceed, you will build the habit of flagging or noticing these feelings so that they will no longer be invisible to you. Only then will you have the opportunity to stop to make sure that you are supporting your well-thought-out resolve.

Anything we do that is different from what we are used to usually feels somehow "not right." These feelings are compounded when we feel the new behavior has been forced on us. But that doesn't mean that the change *is* not right. When we can distinguish what feels "not right" from what is actually not right for us now, and evaluate the situation for ourself, we—not our Silent Partners—are running the show. As we continue to do the new task or to do the task in a new way, it gets easier and easier as we build a new unconscious pattern, because this time it is aligned with our present and current needs rather than with those of the past.

Unfortunately, as with most things, we don't start out doing it perfectly and looking like an expert. It's interesting to note that people who feel the most successful in their life have a harder time acquiring new behaviors. After all, isn't our success a result of the way we have done and thought about things? We have this belief that older people don't or can't change because they are older (as in *old and stubborn*). I have a different theory. Starting something new or doing something in a new way feels the same if you are six or sixty, but when we are younger we expect to be learning many new things. When we are older and have achieved some life mastery, it is not only uncomfortable to feel awkward, it feels demeaning somehow, as if it is "wrong" to not already know. It often seems easier to just do it the old way and put up with the consequences.

After you do this practice exercise and begin to get the hang of it, move on to your short-term goals from chapter 2 (see p. 47). By the way, how many have you already accomplished? Because these are things you want or need to do, but will not automatically accomplish, they are excellent candidates for honing and polishing this new skill. Remember, as you take on each new project, check your other PaperRoom panels to expand your understanding of the other possible connections that might have been strengthening your resistance or can support your ability to follow through. The following list serves as a reminder of items to check.

- Results System (p. 11). Review your Silent Partners' perceptions, beliefs, habits, expectations, and assumptions about the matter.

- "Goals" panel (p. 44). Notice if this new habit or resolve in any way supports your long-range goals.

- "Family" panel (p. 56). Looking at each person separately, is there any connection between your Silent Partners' and your family's way of doing or seeing things, or how you felt your family thought of you, that can shed some light on or support your effort in some way?

- "Patterns" panel (p. 70). Scan the categories in your job history for any clues to your current resistance, or opportunities or reasons that support your new resolve.

- "TopTen" panel (p. 97). What's behind your resistance to change? If the old habit actually is fulfilling one of your core needs or values, you are going to have to either abandon the new habit or find a replacement. You'll need some way to fulfill the need that's supplied by the old habit. How could the desired change benefit you? Is there some way this new way of doing things could fulfill a core need or value?

- Setup reminder (p. 130). Repeat the setup reminder from the previous exercise. If you are having trouble creating a reminder system for yourself, get a partner who can periodically check in with you to keep you on track. Do whatever it takes.

- Just pick a time and do it!

This may sound like a lot of work for a simple task. You're right; it is. But remember, you will not always have to do things like this. You are learning a new skill and then keeping at it long enough for it to become a new, more appropriate, useful Silent Partner. Being annoyed is part of the system that has you repeating the past. As you work to develop this new skill, you are adding a new wrinkle to something you have done in a particular way all your life. Although at times in the past our Silent Partners have undermined us, they also have kept us alive and allowed us to function. We do not want to relearn how to walk every time we wish to move. We don't want to relearn how to drive our car, hold a pencil, or find our desk. We don't want to forget what we already know, but in today's lickety-split changing world, we need to be fluid and nimble so that we can evaluate and embrace the unpredictable as we navigate our career and life. And we want to have the skill to choose self-supporting behaviors rather than those that sabotage our intentions.

Now that you've practiced applying your new skills and tools on a concrete project, and you've sensitized yourself still more to your Silent Partners, you need only put a couple of additional pieces in place before launching into your future. In the next chapter you will broaden the way you're seeing the context of your work/life and future, rid yourself of self-defeating beliefs, and see the broader influence of your life quarter. You will also complete the "New Actions" column of your TopTen chart.

CHAPTER NINE

The Window to Your Future

Everyone looked at me like I had six heads when I started my own business at the age of sixty in a bad economy, but it took off fast. I'd learned about my needs and values, broken the patterns I'd thought were necessary, and redesigned how I was working. It freed me to move into a whole new realm with my business, and a healthy marriage. I'm working essentially part-time, my mind is freer, and my income is the best I've ever had. If you don't jump now you won't find out. The PaperRoom is about taking all you are now and moving forward to capture what you could be if you dared. — Robin

*In this third of four
Action chapters you will:*

- *Review your new tools*
- *Learn the stumbling blocks that could stop you*
- *See more deeply the importance of the second and third quarters*
- *Get some no-nonsense coaching*
- *Complete your TopTen chart*

Free to Move Forward

You've made it this far. Now what? If you have kept to the task, you should have some new results and a lot more insight into how to navigate your career/life more successfully. You should have some answers or at least some movement in the areas you wanted to address when you picked up this book.

Up to now, you've been working with your past and focusing on your current situation, using the "Now" and "Short-Term Goals" panels from chapter 2. It's time now to step back to take the broader view of your future. We want to review your long-term goals—how you envision your life in twenty years. Take out your original "Goals" panel (see p. 44) and check it out.

Does it still look good to you? Does what you planned include things that can fulfill what you have come to identify as your needs and values?

This next-to-last step of the PaperRoom will give you a new context in which to live your life to the fullest. It will help ensure that your current path will predictably lead you to your desired future, your long-term goals. What exactly is it that you would like to address in the coming years? What are your priorities? What will you miss if you don't take the opportunity now? What is the theme, the underpinning of what will matter to you most or make the biggest difference in the quality of your life?

First, we'll review the new tools with which you'll harvest the value from the work you have done to create your new future. Plus, we'll dispose of some of the common mental roadblocks my clients have brought with them to the PaperRoom.

"You've got to know yourself so that you can at last be yourself."
—**D.H. Lawrence, writer**

"Your future depends on many things, but mostly on you."
—**Frank Tyger, author**

Your New Tools

Any carpenter will tell you that the quality of a person's work is directly related to how well he or she knows the tools of the trade. The following are the tools you'll use to begin crafting your career and life over the coming weeks and months. Let's review them so that you have them well in hand. If you are unclear on any of them, refer back to the chapter in which they were introduced. Then, in chapter 10, "Living into Your Future," we offer some suggestions about how you can work with these over time.

- Your Silent Partners (chapters 1, 3, and 8): Understanding, recognizing, and continuing to disempower your Silent Partners (see chapter 8) will enable you to eliminate the self-imposed obstacles that have held you back so you can meet the challenges that are well within your reach.

- TopTen "Core Needs" column (chapter 6): Routinely recognizing your needs and replenishing them, and working with individuals and organizations that share your values, you will be able to perform at your highest level, reaching beyond your self-imposed limits of the past.

- Elliott's Life Domains model (chapter 5): Checking the interplay of your Life Domains and the way their relationships change over time will enable you to keep them in balance. You will want to work with this tool to make temporary adjustments so that you can navigate unexpected upsets when your career/life gets bumpy.

The Broad Lens of Opportunity: The Bigger Picture

"As long as you're going to be thinking anyway, think big!"
—Donald Trump, developer

Now I'd like to have a private, more personal conversation with you about your whole quality of life. The PaperRoom process succeeds because the discoveries we make enable us to make our choices from a broader and deeper perspective. Our new understandings can free us from past limitations, allowing us to make our decisions while looking through an expanded panoramic lens. We have come full circle in this book and are back to our starting point of long-term goals—but you are bringing to the process a new understanding of what it might mean for you to have a full career and life. I want to address here not what you do in your career/life, but the quality of the life you live, which is, of course, affected by your career. Let's look at the entire tapestry you are weaving.

It's No Accident: Life up to Fifty Is the Homework

To look at the whole of your life, we need to give you a deeper understanding of your life quarters, which we introduced in chapter 2. From the PaperRoom's inception, clients tended to go to it when they were at a critical or difficult choice point. Though the patterns of feelings and the frustrations people of each age group were experiencing were similar, the focus for each was different. I noticed a 180-degree shift between how people were measuring their purpose in their early adult years and how they were measuring it later, in their third quarter. As you may remember from chapter 2, in Q2 we try life on and learn to support ourselves and others, establishing ourselves as contributing adults in our communities. We typically compare ourselves to people we know or know of, to learn what is appropriate in life. Around age fifty, at the start of Q3, we begin to evaluate our career wants and needs more by the internal measures we have developed over a lifetime. Trying on jobs, careers, and professions and educating ourselves, learning, succeeding, and failing have already paid off to some degree. We have gathered enough knowledge, experience, and personal understanding to be ready to go after the challenges we have avoided. We become less able to "put up with things" and we are more challenged to have our external world reflect our internal selves. But, regardless of which quarter we are in, the dilemma comes when we know we must step from our old world into the new.

Another thing became clear to me as I listened to my clients. Regardless of what they had done in their earlier adult life, it was in most cases exactly the right "homework" to prepare them for what was to come next. Each life quarter is designed to naturally support the next. So, if you feel anxious in your second quarter about knowing how to make the right choices for the long run, know that whatever you are doing will be useful and valuable in the future. If you are feeling regrets in your third quarter about not having made the right choices along the way, know that whatever you did had value and brought you to where you are now. You, have been preparing for what will come next. The trick when you feel unsure or

"Priorities change. Life comes in segments."
—**Madeleine Albright, former secretary of state**

don't yet see the value in your past choices is, of course, to go with the flow. Nothing is or ever was wasted.

At sixty, I can say that my career is turning out well and I can now appreciate that it wasn't an accident. It is only in retrospect that I can see that the twists and turns of my career were valuable and that most of the major decisions I made at my choice points were the right ones. At the time I was often not clear, nor were the choices always obvious or always pleasant. I did what most of us do; I went with what I believed were the right decisions, or at least the best decisions, for me at the time.

I've heard that, on average, entrepreneurs have ten failures for each success. I haven't had ten business failures, but you could say I have had a most creative "learning curve." When I graduated from high school I went to a junior college for a semester and then quit school and got a job as a receptionist in a retail optical store. After several months, the owner of the store and I agreed that probably I had made a false start and should look elsewhere to begin my career. My next job was as a paste-up artist in an advertising company. I thought that was another false start as well. Between the ages of eighteen and fifty, here are some of the jobs I had:

- Salesperson

- Assistant buyer

- Department manager

- Assistant store manager

- Store manager

- Director of volunteers

- Copresident of the PTA

- Director of advisory board

- Entrepreneur

. . . and some of the things I did:

- Studied tailoring

- Studied fine art

- Studied gourmet cooking

- Assisted at a French cooking school

- Started a company with a backpack that I designed and sold nationally

- Created a corporate catering company

- Cofounded a fresh caviar delivery service

- Consulted for take-out food establishments, a fresh juice factory, a trucking company, and small shops looking to expand or franchise

- Sold candy, clothes, advertising, and personal growth programs

- Led workshops and seminars in personal growth and leadership development

And then, when I was forty-six, I went to college.

Today I can tell you that life up to fifty was exactly the right homework for having the career I really wanted "when I grew up." I didn't know that then, but I know it now. There is truly no way that I could come close to the depth of understanding I bring to the work I do had I not had all that experience. The results in the PaperRoom have shown me that it doesn't matter if you have had eight jobs or more than twenty. It is always exactly the right "homework."

The other thing that I know now and didn't know when I was younger is how important it is to be as true as you possibly can be to your most deeply felt priorities at each stage of your career and life. Regardless of what stage of life you are in, the key to solving your current concern is to be willing to be creative, flexible, tenacious, and rigorous about honoring your own standards and your own deepest knowing of what is right for the moment.

The Deeper Meaning of More Time

Looking at life as having four distinct stages rather than three has broader implications than simply a change of numbers. It not only changes the way we look at our career, it also means that businesses need to look at their workforce differently. It means reassessing how and when managers train and tap talent and for what purpose. It means rethinking how organizations can best use both the new and the seasoned talent in their midst. But guess what? It is not up to them to do it. It is up to us. We are them. This is going to have to be collaboration; we are all in it, and need to be, if it is going to work. Our longer lives are heralding a lifetime of expanded opportunities, a new understanding of the possibilities of what having a career and living a full life mean. We need to shift our attention away from tolerating or coping with the inevitable to taking responsibility for designing a life that is fulfilling, appropriately challenging, and meaningful. The future as we perceived it is not inevitable. We really do have choices. The nature of these choices may vary depending on our time of life, but this expansion of life affects us all, collectively and individually, and calls on us to think in new ways about who we are and how we will succeed.

If I Could Speak with You Personally

If I could speak with you right now, we would have one of those "over a glass of good wine" kinds of conversations where we take a step outside our day-to-day concerns. We would have a very different conversation depending on which life quarter you are in. So rather than bore you with a conversation meant for someone else, I'm going to separate out the two "conversations." One

"We can influence [our future] if we know what we want it to be."
—**Charles Handy, business futurist**

is designed for those in Q2, and a separate one is for those in Q3. If you want to see your life as a balanced whole, then I encourage you to join both.

Q2: Life's Second Quarter

If you believed advertising media's depiction of life from our late twenties to midlife, you'd probably think that Q2 was the most vital and fulfilling of our life quarters. However, the reality may be far less pleasant. I have long thought that our career life in our second quarter is by far the most challenging

So Many Options! In Q2 we are faced with more options than we've ever had, but it is often difficult to feel sure of the basis on which to make our choices. For many of us, just as our career begins to have some real substance and vibrancy, it is time to have children and start a family, if that's our intention. Unlike our feelings in the first throes of the women's liberation movement, now both men and women are seeing the value, the importance, of balancing a rich home life with their career. Yet current wisdom and a fair amount of statistics hold that to pause or slow down our career trajectory for even a short time creates a loss we can never regain. How can we afford that?

The first step is to remember that statistics are based in the past, and the second step is to notice that though you are not a statistic, you are a part of one—a statistic in the making. What you do counts. The third step is to ignore the statistics of the past and create some of our own for the future.

Here's an example of someone who is doing just that. A few years ago I gave a presentation to the Harvard Business School Women's Alumni Association. After my talk, several women came to do the PaperRoom. As friends told friends, there followed a stream of young, bright, educated, frustrated women.

They came to me with a common dilemma: how to balance their investment in, and passion for, their career with their commitment to motherhood. That is how I met Lucinda.

> *Just before I found the PaperRoom, my life was highly in flux—I had a baby, no job, didn't think I would have a job, in touch with a lot of people, but nothing was coming together or clicking. I felt knocked off my horse in a way. Here I was, a Harvard Business School graduate. What was I going to do? I knew I really loved work; it gave me an important validation. But I could see the problems with working full time. It wouldn't be fair to the kids. So I was just trying a lot of different things. I was on a path that wasn't a lot of fun. I learned why later. It didn't leverage what I liked or did best. I never felt, "Oh yeah! I can really get into this!" This was all part of the growing and changing when you have a baby. It's such a shock to your system, your lifestyle; you have to figure that all out.*

And Lucinda went on to invent a lifestyle that took care of herself, her career, and her family. She will tell you exactly how in a minute. For now, I'll tell you that the life she invented was completely consistent with the overarching purpose of her stage of life, her second life quarter.

The Life Purpose of the Second Quarter I have suggested that our purpose in this first chapter of our adulthood is to learn how to master life, to learn what our talent is or can be, and where we fit. We are stepping out into the world, taking on the responsibilities and privileges of being an adult. We learn by doing, by testing ourselves and discovering who we are, by trying on different careers or experiences like clothing, and asking ourselves, "What's me?" We are testing ourselves to see how we do. Our work life is about identifying "the gold" and going for it, whatever that might be. Admittedly, for some of us, "the gold" may at first mean recognizing that we survived our childhood. But at some point we all begin to focus on our external needs for work and family, on our desire to be successful and respected, and on honing our responsibilities as spouses and parents, if we choose that path. It is a quest to find where we fit in the world. These days "the fit" is not readymade, so we need to create it in the way that works best for us. An advantage we have in Q2 is the promise of Q3. Now we can realistically consider having two careers, one that fulfills our needs for now, followed by a new career we love for different reasons beginning in our late forties. Our new life expectancy gives us twenty to twenty-five years to invest in each.

The Q2 Gap I call that terrible time between knowing we need to begin something new and knowing what that thing is "the gap." To me it has always felt like one of those bad dreams where I'm running but can't get anywhere. There is nothing more frustrating, but I have never seen anyone make any major decision without going through it. You can take a little comfort in knowing it is part of the process, it is normal, and the discomfort comes from our intention to get it right.

Here's the good news. It appears that in Q2 you don't need to get it right forever. You just need to get it right *for now*.

Q2's Challenge and Opportunity The challenge and the opportunity is to take advantage of what is important and possible only now, and to figure out how to make it work. Only you know best what that is. You should be in a better position to do that now that you have read this far. You have learned that you have an internal system for doing things that you can learn to use to your advantage, and you have tools to help you recognize and avoid it when it is detrimental. You have learned about your needs and how to recognize and access them, giving you renewed confidence. You are clear about some of the important values you

> "There are admirable potentialities in every human being. Believe in your strength and your youth."
> —**André Gide, author**

"Success in the knowledge economy comes to those who know themselves—their strengths, their values, and how they best perform."
—**Peter F. Drucker, business futurist**

need to share with the people you work with, you have some idea about your work patterns, and you have an expanded awareness of your hidden beliefs and influences. This invaluable knowledge forms the context of your experience. Use it and listen to your head, follow your heart, and assume there are no accidents. Go where the door is open.

An Important Silent Partner: The Glove We have gloves for the cold, gloves for playing golf and driving, gloves for doing the dishes, gloves for getting dressed up, and gloves for gardening. I even had a client who designed gloves for doing housework—different ones for dusting, scrubbing, polishing. We also have a glove for protecting our core self. Having survived our youth, we have learned something about risk and danger. We have acquired some ways to cope with difficult situations and learned to recognize and avoid some of those that could be harmful. This glove only gets more comfortable and flexible as we strive to perform at our highest level, reach beyond what we have limited ourselves to in the past and stretch to discover and fulfill our true potential.

We Have a Few Things Going for Us in Q2 One of the advantages of being in Q2 today is that we are all pioneers in figuring out how to balance our personal and professional lives, how to best take on a work life that will predictably last close to fifty years. We are all striving to redefine the workplace in a rapidly changing and evolving economy. Being thoughtfully creative and innovative about how we design our lives and having a say in how we choose to work is becoming the norm. Being restricted to doing only one thing or staying in one organization is not just rare; it is becoming close to impossible. We are living in a time that is recognized as needing redefinition. Think of the third column on your "Patterns" panel in chapter 4, where you listed all the places you have worked. We had looked at that column to appreciate that everything we do adds to the depth and breadth of our knowledge. Nothing goes to waste. Every new experience makes us more valuable to ourselves and others.

Lucinda is a pioneer in her life, and two of her values are "challenge" and "excellence." Listen to her again, as she tells exactly how she succeeded in being true to her career while raising a family by using her knowledge gained from the PaperRoom.

Now I'm defining what I want to do on my own terms. Before, I'd think, "Gee I hope I can get a job. I wonder what I can get." Now, I'm going to people and saying, "Here's what I can do, and anything that I'd do with you I'd like to do successfully part time, for both of our sakes." There's a lot of common wisdom out there about what's not possible, but you know what? There are a lot of special situations where, if you're looking with a certain perspective, you can find what you want. As a graduate of Harvard Business School, I seek out people who reinforce my thinking. I also built into my plan the support I needed; I helped to form a Harvard Business School moms support group. I created my own support system.

And the way I'm approaching things now, the opportunities have been popping up out of nowhere. I became president of the Harvard Business School Association of Boston, and I decided I was going to hit the ball out of the park on that job. I had a lot of different speakers in, and one was Clay Christianson, author of The Innovator's Dilemma. *During his speech, he blew me away by saying, "If you want to hire somebody great, hire Lucinda." Afterward, somebody came out of the audience and said, "I have a consulting project. Would you like to come talk about it?" If you do something excellent, people think of you for opportunities.*

Now I'm picking the most important work to do and then doing it my absolute best. Before, I was involved in a lot of different things and was giving them equal weight. Now I go for the jewels. In my investment work I decided that I will overdeliver. This was a great way for me to dig in deep and deliver excellent results. I wanted people to say, "When she does something she does a great job." So I really threw myself into it. For me, excellence is more important than breadth. As a direct result of that, one of the people in the group liked my work and said, "I'm starting up a fund, do you want to work with me?"

Lucinda crafted a life that fulfilled her needs and values. Someone whose needs and values included "solitude" and "competence" could design a life equally as successful in its own way. There is no one way, and you can create one that is right for you. That maxim holds true for life in the third quarter as well.

Q3: Life's Third Quarter

Generally Q3 announces itself with emerging feelings of dissatisfaction. Are you becoming a little less tolerant? Do you know that you are not old, but no longer young? Are you aware that you are not ready to quit but painfully clear that your career is no longer fulfilling and that the idea of doing the same work for another twenty years is out of the question? Welcome to Q3.

Is This All There Is? Those of us in our third quarter at around the turn of the millennium are the same people who were the freethinkers of the 1960s and at the forefront of the self-help movement in the late '60s and early '70s. We are accustomed to seeing ourselves as the groundbreakers of new ideas and are familiar with exploring personal growth and change.

Regardless of whether or not you have reached your youthful goals, more than likely you are wondering what's next. Perhaps you are looking forward to a new freedom from family or career responsibilities as children leave home or retirement beckons, but freedom to do what? It becomes clear that you have entered a new life stage, but the only lens you've been given to examine this shift is one that primarily reveals your lost youth or the premature arrival of old age. The transition into the third quarter is labeled "midlife crisis" or "empty-nest syndrome" or simply an unfortunate medical condition. We joke about our losses without recognizing our gains. We have become quite good at noticing what is wrong or needs to be changed, but most of us are not as accomplished at seeing what's right and taking some time out to savor it.

Many of the recent titles about midlife issues reflect the current thinking that midlife is a problem. They address our fears of loss and change—changes in our bodies and in our personal or professional jobs in life, as well as loss of our loved ones, or even of our "faculties." They are primarily reflections on, or suggestions of, how we can live with the change or somehow avoid changing. They come from the core assumption that after fifty the possibility of a useful life is tenuous at best. It seems that the skill that would serve us best is tolerance. That's just nonsense!

To want to stop the world and get off for a moment is not only age appropriate; it is smart and it is normal. To question our assumptions, to explore our needs and values, to stop and take stock of our accomplishments and expectations to reevaluate our future makes good sense. This is not the time of life to follow the leader. There is no right way or one right solution. And, as luck would have it, past learning and experience have prepared us perfectly for this time of life's rich harvest. But first we need to look at the gap between who we were and who we are becoming.

"We did not change as we grew older; we just became more clearly ourselves."
—Lynn Hall, author

The Q3 Gap Many of my current clients are in this difficult place, the gap between knowing how they are going to phase out the "old" career or old way of working and knowing what they are going to do in the "new" one. They are always relieved to know that what they are going through is, if not pleasant, at least normal, and that for many it heralds the culmination of their life's work. In my experience, this is for many a maddeningly long transition. It usually begins sometime in our mid-forties, when we begin to sense that something is amiss, and continues to our mid-fifties before the new life path is clear and begins to take hold. I'm not saying that this entire time is unpleasant. It is simply the sort of transition that we see more clearly for what it is when we find ourselves on the other side.

The Glove Turns Inside Out Our third quarter provides the *opportunity* for the meaningful personal challenges we are only now ready to tackle. We're going for the things that we would later regret not going for. Here is how I like to look at it. Up to this point we have gotten through life by metaphorically wearing a glove. The outer fabric of this glove has protected us from getting hurt. It has allowed us to become, if not always successful, at least relatively adept at surviving the challenges we have faced. The opportunity in Q3 is to turn the glove inside out. I didn't say take it off and be unprotected. I'm suggesting that you simply turn it inside out and let the inner lining show; take the opportunity to dare to do or be or have what you have always wanted.

A few years ago I realized that "turning the glove inside out" had something to do with me as well. It is not an accident that I'm a coach. Coaches have a great role: they get to be an important part of terrific things happening for people, but they are in the background. But my challenge and opportunity has been writing this book with the understanding that I will need to be much more public with the work I do. I have always thought about being more public—I am from Los Angeles after all—but it is not a comfortable role for me. This will be a challenge. But it is a challenge I would regret not having taken if I didn't try.

Q3's Challenge and Opportunity They say that bravery happens when the desire to do something is greater than the fear of doing it. True, but as I've learned, you don't have to do it alone. After fifty or so years you have a pretty good idea about how you want things to be and a fairly decent ability to discern quality; you have the ability to recognize the standard you are looking for when it shows up. You know a lot of people, and you know how to find the ones you don't know. All you need is determination and support for when your bravery flags—which it will.

What I am telling you is that you do not need to know exactly how to do the things you want to do; you already know how to make things happen, and that's all you need. Tap your abundant resources to work out the specifics.

This extension of thirty or so more years of healthy life means that our professional growth doesn't end at fifty and meaningful accomplishment doesn't screech to a halt at sixty-five. At midlife we have the opportunity to start a whole new career if we choose. Here are some examples. In his third quarter, Stephen Spielberg took his career to a whole new level. That talented guy who did the kids' movies turned his glove inside out and made *Schindler's List*. Tom Stemberg "retired" and created Staples office supply stores. Madeleine Albright raised her kids in Q2 and became secretary of state in Q3. Claude Monet did his most important works in his eighties. Longer life means we can have our cake and eat it, too—perhaps even with a bit of frosting.

We Also Have a Few Things Going for Us After living fifty years or so, we have the ability to leverage skills and knowledge honed and refined in our first two quarters. We now have the advantage of hindsight and experience in our personal life. We are neither young nor old. At fifty or so, it becomes necessary to appreciate our strengths, our perceived weaknesses, and the significance of our accomplishments from a new perspective. Only then can we create the career that reflects who we are now and who we can be for the rest of our life. We can take fullest advantage of our third quarter, as Ina has done:

> *I like work but I have to make a conscious decision—it's time for something more. Now I'm managing my time better, making sure that what I go after has a particular quality of life. The first thing is for me to know what I need and want and to own that. And then I balance the time that I have for work, play, and community. I'm navigating my life carefully, knowing what would be good for me, what is healthy for me, meeting the needs that I have. I know it's up to me to take care of myself. And I'm letting go of whatever in my life isn't contributing to me, all those things that are there just because they happen to be there, the things that I didn't choose.*

Q2 and Q3 in Collaboration

We are all at a collective choice point in our world as well as in our businesses and personal lives. Innovations and technology have changed both the possibilities and the very real perils that face us all as human beings. Whether we find ourselves in Q2 or Q3, we may easily overlook what could determine our individual and collective success—our differences. Each quarter brings with it a unique value, which can deepen our understanding, broaden our perspective, and multiply our successes. Q2 people bring energy and the fresh creativity and freedom of a clean slate. Those in Q3 offer wisdom, patience, and experience. Together we are in a far better position to solve the challenges we face as we rethink how and when we work and what kind of work we do. We need to utilize and leverage each other's unique perspective in order to choose wisely.

We now are ready to take the final step to complete your PaperRoom. Shall we?

> *"The great thing about getting older is that you don't lose all the other ages you've been."*
> —Madeleine L'Engle, author

Putting the Final Piece in Place

This personal inquiry will start you on the path to your new career and, ultimately, a new life. You will be employing all the tools and skills you've accrued throughout the book. And, unlike previous exercises, you can work with this one again and again as you move forward. After all, you will continue to change and grow, and now that you know what you know, you will want your career and life to reflect that.

Completing Your TopTen

Refer to the TopTen exercise that you worked on earlier (p. 97) and turn to column 4, "New Actions." The purpose of completing this column is to practice using the TopTen concept so that you will be able to apply it when the time comes. Then later, when you're feeling dissatisfied and have identified the need that needs recharging, you will be able to supply what's missing and again experience yourself as being a healthy, capable person. Go through each TopTen event, remembering how that experience felt. Notice what you said about it and the needs and values it fulfilled. Then think of a new and plausible event that you could have in your work or life that would recreate the missing experience. Remember, for now you're just trying to identify actions that are smaller, simpler, or more easily possible, actions that will enable you to recreate for yourself the experience of each TopTen event. I've included some examples and explanations in the "TopTen Sample" (pp. 154–155) to assist you.

The final chapter, "Living into Your Future," will support you in your continued success. Use the tools and exercises at a frequency that works best for you.

MY TOPTEN	WHY?	CORE NEEDS
1 Family trip to Providence	→ Exploring and discovering things together	Connection: accomplishment and discovery
2 White-water trip	→ Beautiful, spectacular community	Accomplishment, challenge, connection
3 Walking through the fields at my grandmother's house	→ Safety, my spot, freedom →	Connection, individualization
4 Having my children	→ Huge change to something I felt confident/competent about; sense of accomplishment; partnership	Beginnings; connection; recognition
5 Falling in love	→ New beginning—feeling it would be there forever	Beginnings; recognition; connection; accomplishment
6 The road trip with Mark	Camaraderie; closeness; "real talk," really got to know him, changed our relationship forever	Connection, discovery; recognition

ACTIONS

_____

t new restaurant
   Joan

metal sculpture

ffice door, opening
not doing a

un the Book Fair

anta Fe!

d a call... go see
to the museum

In order to repeat the kind of satisfaction we need at a particular time, we must be able to repeat the kind of experience it was. The five examples of connection at left are all slightly different from one another.

In the first example, it was a connection to and with "family." Ellen and Joan are not this person's blood relatives—but they feel like family to her. Going to the new restaurant that they had all been wondering about "felt" the same to her as exploring Providence with her cousins had.

In the second example, the connection that is important in the white-water trip is the friendships this individual had made with a new group sharing a common interest. To an outsider, a sculpting class might not seem anything like the exciting white-water rafting trip, but having new friends who appreciate and can discuss the challenges of metalwork is the same!

In our third example, walking through grandmother's field was a connection to family and to self. It was realizing that remembering to take a few moments to close the office door, turn off the telephone, "merely" to stare out the window was all that was needed to reconnect with oneself and gain a fresh perspective.

Would you think that "moving to Santa Fe, New Mexico," is anything like falling in love? Maybe not, but for this individual it is. This client was an unmarried Hispanic woman working in Michigan. When we discussed what might give her the same sort of experience that she could create, she realized it contained "the feeling it would be there forever" and the experience of "coming home" and not being an outsider. She needed to be with people she felt more culturally connected to.

In our fifth example, we see the simple need to be in contact with a close friend. Here is a senior executive who doesn't feel he has much opportunity to speak his mind and have others freely speak theirs. For the most part, that's fine, but sometimes he really has a need to connect with someone with whom he can have a "real talk" about people, things, and interests that are apart from his work life.

CHAPTER TEN

Living into Your Future

Since I did the PaperRoom, I've been using it to navigate all the changes in my life. These tools are working tools for life. I do a PaperRoom check-in every few months, and things I've learned about myself in the PaperRoom come to mind all the time. I rework the exercises, especially when I'm heading into another change of any kind. Right now, I'm about to start looking for a new job, so I'm focusing on my needs and values to be sure that I will find a good fit. I'm updating my timeline, and I keep a chart of my Life Domains on the wall beside my desk. It's amazing the insights that come to me just by glancing at it. — Wayne

In this fourth of four
          Action chapters you will:

• Get some important advice and coaching

• Learn how your Life Domains can keep working
  for you

• Track your life with your Timeline of Needs
  and Values

• Learn a new level of housecleaning that will keep
  you free to move forward

Maintaining Stability

According to Alan Cohen in his book *Living from the Heart,* in a certain African tribe everyone has a song of his or her own that's sung at all important events and passages of that person's life. The first time people hear their song is at their birth; next when they start school; then at their initiation into adulthood. The next time is when they marry, and finally, at the end of their life, their family and tribe sing them into their next life. There is one other time a person might hear his or her song. If at any time the person displays antisocial behavior, or somehow goes against the norms of the tribe, the community gathers around and sings his or her song, the idea being that punishment is not necessary when we remember who we are. Unfortunately, in our culture we have no such formal (or gentle) personal reminders, but timely reviews of our own design will certainly work as well.

At the end of the Progress Path of Change we reach the plateau called "stability." Unfortunately, without some sort of uncomfortable reminder, the way we usually relate to stability is, "Great, I don't need to think about that now," rather than, "It's okay; it just needs periodic maintenance and adjustment." We may not have grown up in an African tribe that sings to us at important life transitions and reminds us when we falter, but we do know when things are somehow not right and we are not living true to ourselves. We realize that we chose the wrong path or found that for some reason the path we were on came to an end. That's when we know a choice point has arrived.

This chapter contains exercises that will keep you on your path into your future. You will want to return to them, rework them, and check in with them from time to time. You may try a regular schedule or you may feel you would rather wait until you notice you're feeling a bit off track. The right pace for refreshers will become evident to you. You will know you're doing it right if each time you return you learn something new or see a new opening, a new possibility for choice. Each time you learn, you can be assured that you are keeping up with your life as it evolves, that you are living into your future rather than struggling to maintain your past.

Transitions

There is an old story about an Alaskan stone carver who created wonderful sculptures of Alaskan wildlife. When he was asked how he learned to carve so beautifully, he answered that there was nothing much to learn; he just chipped away until the polar bear emerged. If the passage to each time of life were something

What usually signals to you that you have reached a choice point?

———————————

———————————

———————————

———————————

———————————

"May you live all the days of your life."
—Jonathan Swift, author

that we could learn, the challenge would be less difficult. But like the stonecutter's work, this is a methodical and random chipping away of all that is inauthentic or extraneous so that our true selves can emerge.

Advice for Life

Here is some advice to help you make your passage with the greatest skill and ease.

Do It While You Can One day, our friend Frank was discussing something he was thinking about doing with his dad, and his father's response was, "Do it while you can, Frank." At the time we thought it was so funny, so "significant" sounding. What was the big deal? If we don't do it now, there's always later . . . right?

Take Charge of the Future Many of the people I have worked with over the years have found new and creative ways to have careers that differ from the traditional one-job, five-day-workweek norm. Must you have only one job in the five or so days that you would like to work each week? Must all your jobs be paying jobs, or must they all pay the same? Must you really work at them all year long? What do you really need or want at this point in your life? How should it look? Because the possibilities that our second and third quarters hold are yet to be discovered culturally as well as individually, we have more questions than answers. The exploration has just begun. The exercises in this chapter will support you as you move forward in your exploration. I encourage you to review them periodically, refining your answers and celebrating your successes.

Business futurist Charles Handy said, "The way you make sense of the future, in organizations, in societies, and in your own life, is by taking charge of the future, not by responding to

"Don't be afraid your life will end; be afraid that it will never begin."
—Grace Hansen, politician

"Be on the alert to recognize your prime at whatever time of your life it may occur."
—Muriel Spark, author

it." Handy actually practices this. He spends part of the year writing at his rural home; during the remainder of the year, he travels and gives speeches. "That's fine for him," you might say. "He is famous and has a choice." Maybe. My experience with clients has demonstrated that regardless of their success, or perhaps even because of their success, many feel locked into an "all or nothing" frame of mind that limits them to "I have to keep doing what I am doing or quit altogether."

Get Back on the Horse This old adage is certainly true. But in light of the new information you have just learned, here is a point you may not have considered. Getting back on the horse is a step into the future, not the past, and each time we do it, it gets easier. We become more facile and have more grace. In a very short time our new Silent Partners learn to take over without even a pause. You need only to see a professional athlete quickly move beyond the missed jump, or ball, or hoop to appreciate the process. The fall is simply part of the ride—to learn from it, integrate it into your experience, not get stopped by it, and move on seamlessly.

Don't Rely Solely on Practical Considerations Having a "balanced life" is a multidimensional thing. It means a comfortable and effective balance between work and play, which includes both challenging and easy endeavors in addition to those that are necessary and those that are just for fun. They weren't kidding when they said, "All work and no play makes Jack a dull boy."

Risk, but Don't Be At Risk In chapter 1 we talked about the effectiveness of our Silent Partners' ability to keep us in the past by having us feel that something is wrong when we do things differently. There is just no way to continue to grow and mature without feeling that we are at risk. Our job is to make sure this

> *"This thing that we call 'failure' is not the falling down, but the staying down."*
> —**Mary Pickford, actress**

> *"Take calculated risks. That is quite different from being rash."*
> —**George S. Patton, U.S. Army general**

is only a feeling by continuing to check the evidence—making sure that nothing of value is really in jeopardy, that we have solid contingency plans in place and are prepared for the possibility that our plan will not work out, or will not work out as planned.

Coaching for Your Success

The bottom line of what I want to tell you, the very best coaching I can give you, is to follow the intelligence of your heart—or your gut. Do what you know needs to be done and "go where the door is open." My personal experience and the evidence I've gathered from my professional work lead me to believe that optimally navigating career and life together is a partnership of sorts between opportunity and desire. Choose the opportunity available to you that you want to have and trust that it will work out. There will be losses, some anticipated, some not. Trust that it is somehow all part of the plan and that you really can have what you want, though it might not look exactly as you envisioned it.

Here's your final personal inquiry, which will support you into your future.

Charting Your Progress

Your Life Domains and your timeline evolve as you do. They are mirrors of who you are and what's important to you. They are the reflections of your progress that will give you the clarity necessary for living a life that is true to you. Add to that a periodic house-cleaning of your experience of your life and you will be free to move forward. These three tools, with regular use, will be your guides and supports in your ongoing journey.

Step 1: Continual Learning from Your Life Domains

Let's start by looking at how you can continue to work with and rework your Life Domains. As you may recall, Elliott's model in chapter 5 shows that our domains are "capped" or deeply influenced by our spirituality, however we define it, and our mental and physical health and well-being. Locate these two areas at the top and bottom of the pie chart on page 164.

These factors affect our creativity and communication, which affect our relationship with our:

- Personal development

- Spirituality

- Finance

- Vocation/avocation

- Health and well-being

- Family and community

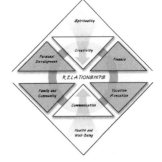

The energy that drives those relationships comes from communication and creativity. We each have all these things in our life at all times, but at any given moment one or two may be more important or more troubling than the others.

As you move toward your goals and set new ones, your Life Domains will shift and evolve in tune with those goals. So you will want to return here on a regular basis. Determine what frequency will support you in maintaining forward motion. As you look deeper into what these domains mean to you, notice how they affect each other. Begin to notice what is true for you.

Does your personal development impact your spirituality? How? Does your vocation impact your health? How much?

Each domain impacts another in some way, and you have a relationship to each domain. Notice what your relationship is to your finances, your vocation and avocations, your health, and so forth. Any fine-tuning needed there?

Examining How You Spend Your Time

Now that you've examined each of your Life Domains and the relationships between them, you can begin to examine what you can actually do about allocating your time to specific areas. Create a pie chart to show how much time you dedicate to each of your Life Domains on a monthly basis. Then think about the following questions and jot down some notes that will help you begin to focus on where you spend your time.

Does a domain that looked relatively unimportant achieve higher importance because of its impact on other domains?

_____

_____

Do you see that you need to give one area more or less attention?

_____

How Am I Going to Spend My Time?   Activity / Goal

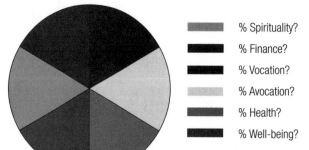

	Activity / Goal
▬▬	% Spirituality?
▬▬	% Finance?
▬▬	% Vocation?
▬▬	% Avocation?
▬▬	% Health?
▬▬	% Well-being?

DIRECTIONS
- Color code area of focus to match color used on the chart
- Fill in targeted activity or goal if desired
- Delegate % of time to be used for this activity

What do you see that you had not seen before?

_____

Jackie's Life Domains exercise, shown in the following pie charts, will help you. Use the steps she followed in her exercise to create a chart that reflects where you spend your time. Then create a second chart reflecting how you'd prefer to spend it. In conjunction with this, you may want to start a Life Domains journal. It can be fascinating and illuminating to read what you thought a year or two ago.

When you have completed your new pie chart, take some time to map out how you are going to accomplish any changes you need to make. You might want to refer back to chapter 8, "Working the System," to set up a game plan.

Current Life Domains Pie Chart

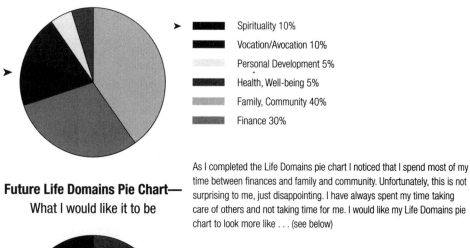

- Spirituality 10%
- Vocation/Avocation 10%
- Personal Development 5%
- Health, Well-being 5%
- Family, Community 40%
- Finance 30%

As I completed the Life Domains pie chart I noticed that I spend most of my time between finances and family and community. Unfortunately, this is not surprising to me, just disappointing. I have always spent my time taking care of others and not taking time for me. I would like my Life Domains pie chart to look more like . . . (see below)

Future Life Domains Pie Chart—
What I would like it to be

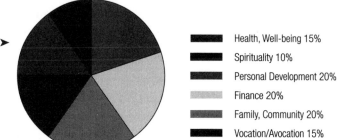

- Health, Well-being 15%
- Spirituality 10%
- Personal Development 20%
- Finance 20%
- Family, Community 20%
- Vocation/Avocation 15%

Step 2: Reviewing Choice Points—Your Timeline of Needs, Values, and Life Domains

A timeline can become an interactive tool that will enable you to step back periodically to review your life in some way. You will actually see the progression of your life as it affects your career. When you feel bound up in the present or find yourself in "the gap," looking over your timeline will remind you how far you have come and get you back in touch with the big picture.

Tracking the Times of Your Life

A timeline template is provided here and is also downloadable at *www.thepaperroom.com*. You may notice that you had little or no choice in regard to the events earlier in your life. Then, at some point, you began to make more choices for yourself. Beneath the earlier significant events, write down the needs or values learned from each experience. Beneath the later events that were more clearly choices you made, write the needs or values that prompted the choice. Why was that choice important for you? If you need a little help defining your needs or values, refer back to the discussion of core needs in chapter 6 with its definitions of *challenge, recognition, accomplishment,* and *connection.* Be as clear as you can about why you made each choice along the way, and put down a word or two. The sample timeline on p. 167 may be of help.

Along the timeline, note which of your Life Domains was most important at each stage of your life. Each time you return to your timeline to update it, notice any shifts in priorities that have occurred and which needs and values are now being fulfilled.

Step 3: Keeping Your House in Order

Here we move beyond the physical housecleaning that we did in chapter 5. We move from our physical space to the realm of our experience. Now that you've completed your TopTen, you are equipped to define the elements you need to be comfortable in a particular work environment. To be happy in your career, you'll want to work in an environment where your most important TopTen needs are met. The others you can satisfy though community involvement, hobbies, or other outlets. Choose the environment in which you can take advantage of the greater time (space) available to you to really focus on what is important in your life at this time.

You may think it's necessary to find a new environment to do this, but before you leap, ask yourself if you actually need to change jobs or if you can set things up a bit differently for your cur-

Life Quarters Choice Points

**Q1: Youth
(1-25)**

Theme: Education
Purpose: Learning the
   ropes of life
Job: Finding our place
   in society

**Q2: Adult
(25-50)**

Theme: Creation and
   stability
Purpose: Providing for
   ourselves and future
   generations
Job: Building the future

**Q3: Mentor
(50-75)**

Theme: Contribution &
   community
Purpose: Authenticity
Job: Fulfilling who we know
   ourselves to be

**Q4: Historian
(75-100)**

Theme: Treasurers of the past;
   keepers of history
Purpose: Ensuring the continuum
Job: Teaching and sharing our
   historical perspective
   and wisdom

0

25

50

75

100

rent job to be more fulfilling. Or conversely, is this the time to move out of your comfort zone to risk doing something different?

On a new piece of paper, with your list of needs and values at hand, respond to the following questions. As you do, bear in mind that you are doing a housecleaning of your way of thinking here as well. Are there:

- Ways you could rethink your present job?

- Ways you could build in the elements you need?

- Ways you could divest yourself of aspects of your job that no longer serve you?

- Conversations you could have with others that would make a difference?

Also, can you:

- "Clean up" or correct misunderstandings?

- Express avoided apologies?

- Extend overlooked thank-yous?

- Give well-earned acknowledgments?

This is the same kind of housecleaning I suggest for people leaving one job for another. You want to leave everything in perfect shape, relationships intact, and projects complete to open the space for new things to flourish. You can use this same review and closure if you leave your current position literally or figuratively. After all, you are looking to change the current situation and start fresh. Imagine that it's possible to recreate your current job to support your present values. Begin thinking about what sort of housecleaning that would take.

If it doesn't look possible to recreate your present job, you may want to begin to write the formula for a job that would fulfill your needs and values. What would it look like? At the bottom of your sheet, list the job, career, and work environment criteria for success based on your needs and values. Include all elements that are important to you. These might include:

- Degree of autonomy

- Self-employment or employment by an organization

- Size of organization

- Organizational values

- Organizational environment

- Kind of boss

- Type of role (support, leadership, facilitator)

Guidelines for Staying on Track

Set up a way to permanently stay on track. This might mean creating a support group, as Lucinda and I have each done, or it could be a regularly scheduled periodic review on your own. One client who started with me years ago comes regularly to discuss and target new results in five areas of his life in the upcoming business quarter. I have several clients who see me every six months, and a few I see regularly once a year for this purpose. What can you set up that will support you? It can be as easy as just putting a note on your calendar if that will work for you.

Congratulations! You have now completed the PaperRoom process. You have learned about your Results System and Silent Partners. You know your core needs and values. You are more aware of your potential pitfalls and know how to avoid them, and have some long-term goals and tools to support your reaching them. You have a new way to look at the trajectory of your career/life and a deeper understanding about how to make wise personal choices. As your life continues to grow and change, refer back to this or any of the other exercises as you reach new choice points.

I wish you well as you encounter each new life stage and each new choice point reveals itself. Have a wonderfully rich and satisfying career, and above all, a life that is a true expression of you, and all that you can be.

Guidelines for Starting a Book Group

The Setup

The opportunity to benefit from others' perspectives, support, and camaraderie will magnify and deepen your discoveries and results. The following guidelines offer a way to help you form and run a successful group. As you work together, you can modify the way the group is organized so that it works best for you.

Group composition: To ensure the comfort level and freedom of speech needed for this work, consider meeting outside the workplace with people who are not part of your work community.

Group size: Three to five people is a good size. You will want to have enough people to get a few other perspectives about the material being discussed, but some of the chapters will generate so much material that it will take too long to discuss it with as many as six people.

Prior to Your First Meeting

To get off to the best possible start, before your first meeting all group members should read the following:

- The introduction

- Chapter 1

- The first meeting guidelines on pages 172–173

Materials Needed

- A notebook: You will need a notebook to answer the personal inquiry questions in each chapter, and you might want to leave room for taking notes at your meetings (by chapter) as well

- A copy of this book

First Meeting: Suggested Guidelines to Preserve Personal Comfort of Members

In many ways your first meeting will set the context or tone for your future meetings, and it will be important to start off on the right foot—so in many ways this will be a business meeting. The following are suggestions you may find helpful.

1. **Design a meeting agenda format.** You will need time to catch up on things that were left open from the last meeting and make any adjustments to this meeting's agenda depending on the material to be discussed and/or the number of those attending this meeting. You will want some balance between individuals' discoveries, concerns, and questions, as well as time to discuss the current topic as a group.

2. **Designate a timekeeper.** In the beginning it will be useful to have a timekeeper to help keep you on track. Later it may not be as necessary as you fall into a workable pattern allowing everyone time to speak.

3. **Create a confidentiality agreement.** *Confidentiality* is one of those words that we all think we know the meaning of, but often discover that we have different understandings about what, exactly, it means. Please have this discussion in the group and make sure that you are all in agreement about what is and is not acceptable, so that all feel

that their privacy is maintained within the group. Like many personal discovery processes, the more honest you can be, the better results you will get, so it is important to feel as safe as possible with your group members.

4. **Speak.** The value and purpose of sharing your thoughts and discoveries with a group is to get people's perspective and feedback about the situation you are discussing. Often others see or hear things differently than we do. The group members' job is to reflect back any insights or questions they may have about the material you are discussing to give you new ways to see the information and expand your perspective. Here are some good basic rules:

- Everyone should speak in the first person, using "I" statements, e.g., "What I hear you saying is . . . ," "I'm noticing that . . . ," etc.

- Everyone should listen respectfully and nonjudgmentally.

- Nothing spoken of in the group is to be brought up outside the group without permission.

- One person speaks at a time and only at his or her designated time or during group chats.

Suggested First Meeting Agenda

This is a general outline for an agenda based on a five-person, two-hour group meeting that should work for you for starters. It is by no means carved in stone. Each of our test groups for the book ultimately designed some variation on this theme for its permanent agenda.

- Allow each person time to share his or her thoughts about why he or she wanted to be in this group and his or her expected results from this experience (3 min. each, 15 min. total)

- Decide on timekeeper(s)—those responsible for moving the group along—for future meetings (note to timekeeper: five- and two-minute "warnings" are often useful until individuals get used to how long they can speak) (5 min.)

- Discuss and find agreement on confidentiality (30 min.)

- Share reactions to the chapter currently being discussed (25 min.)

- Share answers to personal inquiry homework (5 min. each, 25 min. total)

- Set up future meeting times and dates and conduct open chats (20 min.)

Note: It is useful to decide how you want to handle attendance. It is predictable that from time to time someone will not be able to make a meeting. Like everything else in life, take your best shot at what you think will work best and be flexible.

The *www.thepaperroom.com* Web site has additional information for people wanting to start PaperRoom work groups.

Index